BEYOND EXPECTATIONS

Empowering Home-Makers to Rewrite their Story and Lead Extraordinary Lives

By Farida Bharmal

Book Creation Services

by

BookMyStory

It's time to tell your story

www.bookmystorypublishing.com

A venture of

R&S Enterprises

BEYOND EXPECTATIONS
Farida Bharmal

Published by Qurate Books Pvt. Ltd.

Published in 2023

ISBN: 978-93-5898-076-9

Qurate
quratebooks.com

Qurate Books Pvt. Ltd.
Goa 403523, India
www.quratebooks.com
Tel: 1800-210-6527, Email: info@quratebooks.com

DEDICATION

Dedicate this book to My Mentor, My Mariyam Ma, My Farida Ma, and all those amazing women who want to live an extraordinary life

GIFT

🎉 Thank You for Choosing "Beyond Expectations"! 📚

Dear Readers,

I am Farida Bharmal, a Business and Mindset Coach, as well as an Expert in Graphology. I want to express my heartfelt gratitude for choosing "Beyond Expectations" as your reading companion. Your support means the world to me, and I'm thrilled to have you on this journey of personal growth and empowerment.

As a special gift, I'd like to offer you access to two FREE videos that can significantly impact your personal growth journey:

1. **"10 Habits That Make You Mentally Weak"**
Learn to identify and overcome the habits that may be holding you back from your full potential.

2. **"How to Develop Mental Strength"**
Discover practical strategies to build resilience and mental fortitude.

To access these videos, simply scan the QR code below:

These videos are designed to complement the lessons and insights you've gained from "Beyond Expectations." They are my way of saying thank you and providing you with additional tools to empower yourself.

Thank you once again for your incredible support. I hope you find these videos valuable on your journey toward personal and mental growth.

I wish you continued success and empowerment!

Best regards,
Farida Bharmal
Business and Mindset Coach
Expert in Graphology (Handwriting Analysis)

PREFACE

Dear Resourceful Nurturers,

Welcome to **Beyond *Expectations "Empowering Home-Makers to Rewrite their Story and Lead Extraordinary Life's"*** within these pages, you will embark on a transformative journey alongside growth-minded homemakers, like yourself, who yearn to reclaim their identity, embrace their authority, conquer fear, and make empowered decisions.

This book is a labour of love, driven by a deep desire to uplift and support those who have dedicated themselves to creating warm and nurturing homes. As an expert in guiding homemakers on their path to personal growth, I have witnessed the extraordinary challenges they face in navigating their roles and responsibilities. It is with profound empathy and unwavering purpose that I present to you the reasons that compelled me to write this book.

First and foremost, your incredible resilience has inspired me. Despite the inherent complexities of your roles, you selflessly pour your hearts into your families, often sacrificing your own dreams and aspirations. I felt a calling to empower you to reclaim your sense of self and find fulfilment beyond your domestic responsibilities.

Secondly, I have been deeply moved by your stories of feeling disconnected and losing yourselves in the daily chaos of life. This book seeks to provide you with the tools and guidance needed to reclaim your personal agency and shape your own destinies, to rediscover the essence of who you truly are.

Thirdly, I firmly believe that every person possesses unique gifts and untapped potential waiting to be unlocked. You, as homemakers, harbour talents and passions that deserve to be discovered and celebrated. By helping you identify your strengths and cultivate your individuality, we can unleash a wave of personal growth and empowerment that will positively impact your lives and those around you.

Moreover, witnessing the profound transformation experienced by those who have embraced their own identities has been an incredible inspiration. I have had the privilege of witnessing individuals who were once overshadowed and overlooked rise to become confident, assertive, and accomplished. Their stories serve as a testament to the power of self-discovery, and I am honoured to share their wisdom with you.

Finally, I believe that the world greatly benefits from the unique perspectives and contributions of empowered homemakers. By stepping into your own authority and making decisions aligned with your values and aspirations, you have the potential to create profound positive change in your families, communities, and beyond. This book aims to equip you with the necessary tools and mindset to make an impact and leave a lasting imprint on the world.

In conclusion, "Beyond Expectations" is a heartfelt endeavour aimed at guiding growth-minded home makers like yourself toward self-empowerment, authenticity, and the fulfilment of your dreams. Together, let us embark on a path of self-discovery, breaking free from limitations and embracing the transformative power within.

With warm regards,

Farida Bharmal

The Phoenix's Tale: A Story of Reinvention

I have a deep love for reading, and my introduction to the concept of the phoenix came through the pages of the "Harry Potter" series. It was there that I first encountered this mythical bird, and its story of rebirth and transformation left an indelible mark on my imagination. This narrative struck a chord with me, igniting the idea of using the phoenix as a central symbol on our book's cover.

Just as Harry Potter and his world were touched by the phoenix's remarkable qualities, I envisioned our readers experiencing a similar sense of renewal and transformation within the pages of our narrative. The phoenix, with its ability to rise from its own ashes, became the embodiment of the empowerment journey we wished to convey. Its vivid and fiery presence on the cover signifies the passion, determination, and the unwavering commitment required to rediscover one's true identity amidst the complexities of life. The idea is that even if everything is over, one shouldn't lose hope no matter what.

The phoenix's expansive wings are a potent symbol of the freedom to rise above challenges, take command of one's destiny, and assert personal authority. It is a reminder that, like the phoenix, our readers have the innate capacity to rise, transform, and embrace their destinies. This connection between the phoenix and our narrative is a testament to the profound power of literature and storytelling. It's a reminder that the magic of a great story can ignite the spark of transformation and empowerment. This is why I chose to incorporate the phoenix into our cover design, as a symbol that encapsulates the essence of our journey, inspiring us all to rise and transform.

INTRODUCTION

I am Farida Bharmal, the founder of Meerakii Counselling and Training Centre. My passion lies in empowering women to live their dream lives, and I have dedicated over a decade to counselling, graphology, and mindset coaching. As an award-winning Graphologist, I analyse handwriting to unlock hidden insights, and as a certified counsellor and Mindset Coach, I guide women toward personal and professional growth. Throughout my journey, I've had the privilege of empowering more than 15,000 educated, growth-minded women. My mission is to help them become confident, competent, and financially independent.

I am also proud to be a co-author of two transformative books, "I Am - Disaster to Master" and "I Am - Mess to Messenger," which have touched countless lives with their messages of resilience and growth. With my motivational and easy-to-understand approach, I have become a guiding light personality designer for women seeking to create an impact in their personal and professional lives. Together, let us embark on a journey towards living our dream lives and empowering ourselves to become the best versions of who we truly are.

TABLE OF CONTENTS

INTRODUCTION

Unleash Your Hidden Power: 7 Proven Steps to Empower Growth-Minded Home Makers and Transform Your Life!

Hey there, charming ladies! Are you ready to ignite the fire within you and embark on a life-altering journey? If you're nodding your head and craving a life filled with purpose, where you can build your identity, fearlessly make decisions, and claim the power to shape your own destiny, then you've stumbled upon the key to unlocking your true potential.

Imagine a life where you wake up each day, bursting with enthusiasm and drive. Picture yourself standing tall, radiating confidence, and leaving a positive impact on those around you. This book is your ticket to that extraordinary life—a life where you, as a growth-minded homemaker, take charge and create a future brimming with success and fulfilment.

So, what's the secret sauce? It's a 7-step process tailor-made for someone just like you—someone who is ready to break free from the chains that bind and rewrite their story. Each step is carefully crafted to guide you toward building your identity, nurturing your authority, making fearless decisions, and embracing a life of abundance and positivity.

Step 1: Empowering Yourself for Personal Growth and Independence

First things first, let's uncover that incredible potential within you. We'll dive into self-care, goal setting, and cultivating a growth mindset. Together, we'll lay a rock-solid foundation for your personal growth and independence. Get ready to unleash your inner strength and believe in your ability to achieve greatness.

Step 2: Cultivating Meaningful Relationships and Connections

You know what they say: no one succeeds alone. We'll explore the power of building authentic relationships and connections that support and inspire you. Surround yourself with a tribe of like-minded individuals who believe in your dreams. Together, we'll create an unstoppable force that propels you towards success.

Step 3: Prioritizing Well-being and Finding Balance in Your Life

Life can be a juggling act, but it's time to find balance and prioritize your well-being. We'll uncover strategies to care for your physical, emotional, and mental health, ensuring you have the energy and clarity to conquer any challenges that come your way. You deserve to thrive in all aspects of your life.

Step 4: Overcoming Challenges and Embracing Fearlessness

Ah, challenges—they're simply stepping stones in disguise. We'll equip you with powerful techniques to overcome obstacles and embrace fearlessness. No longer will setbacks hold you back. With a fearless spirit and a mindset primed for success, you'll rise above any challenge and forge your own path.

Step 5: Building a Supportive Network and Engaging in Community

Community is everything, my friend. Together, we'll unlock the potential of building a supportive network that propels you forward. Discover the joy of collaboration and the power of lifting others up. By sharing your knowledge and experiences, you'll create a ripple effect of positive change and open doors you never thought possible.

Step 6: Achieving Financial Freedom and Security

Empowerment reaches beyond personal growth—it extends to your financial well-being too. We'll delve into effective financial management, budgeting, and investing. Unleash your financial prowess and create a solid foundation that gives you the freedom to pursue your dreams and enjoy a life of abundance.

Step 7: Nurturing a Mindset of Abundance and Positivity

Last but certainly not least, it's time to nurture a mindset of abundance and positivity. We'll tap into the transformative power of gratitude, visualization, and affirmations. Get ready to attract limitless possibilities and create a life that exceeds even your wildest dreams.

Within the pages of this remarkable book, you will find an intimate companion, guiding you every step of the way. Together, we will conquer the limitations that have held you back, unleashing the incredible power that lies within you. Brace yourself for a life-altering experience as we rewrite the script of your existence, paving the path to the life you've always yearned for. This is your chance to claim the extraordinary, to tap into your deepest aspirations, and to seize the reins of your destiny. Don't hesitate - the adventure begins now!

Are you ready to take the leap? Join me, and let's embark on this thrilling adventure together. Your transformation starts now!

From Ordinary to Extraordinary:

Home Makers Redefining Success

"Overcome the fear of judgment and criticism. Step out of your comfort zone and embrace your unique journey. Your voice and choices matter."

Buckle up, because we're about to dive headfirst into the challenges that await you on the path to building your identity, being fearless, and taking your own decisions. Now, you might be wondering, why should you pay attention to these challenges. Why not just focus on the end goal?

Well, my dear fellow homemakers, the truth is that challenges are the catalysts for growth. They are the stepping stones that lead us to greatness. Each hurdle you encounter on this journey is an opportunity for self-reflection, personal development, and unlocking your true potential.

By paying attention to these challenges, you gain valuable insights into yourself and the world around you. You uncover hidden strengths, resilience, and determination you never knew existed. Embracing these obstacles with open arms allows you to cultivate a mindset of growth and resilience, propelling you towards a life of fulfilment and empowerment.

Remember, a diamond is formed under pressure. Just like that precious gem, you have the power to transform the challenges you face into opportunities for brilliance. Each challenge conquered becomes a testament to your strength, courage, and unwavering spirit.

By acknowledging and understanding these challenges, you equip yourself with the tools and knowledge needed to overcome them. You become a warrior, armed with the wisdom gained from your experiences. With this newfound understanding, you can navigate the hurdles with grace and determination, never allowing them to hold you back from reaching your full potential.

Allow me to share one conversation I had with a progress-minded Home Maker who wanted to build her identity and be an independent and autonomous decision-maker.

During our heartfelt conversation, the fearless homemaker bared her soul, sharing the pains and challenges she faces on her journey to build her identity and reclaim her autonomy. Her voice trembled as she expressed the weight of societal expectations and the constant struggle to strike a delicate balance between her responsibilities and personal aspirations. Tears welled up as she spoke about the nagging self-doubt and the paralyzing fear of failure that often clouded her path. Yet, amidst her vulnerability, a flicker of determination emerged, illuminating her words as she vowed to take small steps toward personal growth and self-discovery. With a voice filled with longing, she yearned for a supportive community of like-minded individuals who could lift her spirits and understand her deepest desires.

In that moment of realization, I was struck by the profound sense of isolation within a bustling community. Our souls long for nourishment, our buried desires yearn to be unleashed, yet they often take a backseat to what society deems more important. Our time slips away, our emotions go unexpressed or misunderstood, and our voices fade into the background. It was then that I witnessed the smouldering anger and frustration within these remarkable women. I saw the untapped spark awaiting ignition, craving recognition and nurturing.

But what, I pondered, stands in the way of us embracing our vibrant, extraordinary selves? After countless conversations with over 500 women, I have identified common barriers that hold us back. Let us now explore each one, reframing them and kick them out of our lives once and for all.

1. Cultural Expectations and Stereotypes:

I have heard so many growth-oriented homemakers tell me, “Farida, it's truly challenging when society imposes predefined roles on us solely because we are women. We often feel pressured to prioritize our family's needs over our personal ambitions, which can create a conflict within ourselves. However, deep down, we long to break free from these limitations and chart our own course in life. It's an internal journey, a quest to embrace our true identity and live authentically while honouring the value of family and tradition that is important to us. How do we do justice to both ?”

Navigating cultural expectations and stereotypes poses challenges for growth-oriented homemakers. Balancing personal aspirations amidst societal norms, facing judgment and criticism, and feeling the pressure to conform can hinder their progress.

2. Lack of Support:

Ladies, it's not easy when the people around us don't understand or support our dreams. Sometimes our own families don't believe in us, and it can be disheartening. We need that cheerleader in our corner, someone who believes in us and encourages us to grow. It's like having a lifeline to keep us going.

3. Balancing Multiple Roles:

Oh, my goodness !! finding a balance between being a wife, and a mother, and managing everything at home is like walking a tightrope. It feels like we're being pulled in a million different directions, and it's hard to find time for ourselves. We want to pursue our own passions and dreams, but it's tough to juggle everything without feeling guilty.

4. Limited Exposure and Opportunities:

You know, sometimes it feels like we're stuck in a bubble, and we don't have the same chances as others. We want to learn new things, maybe go back to school or explore different careers, but it's not always easy. We have so much untapped potential, and we want the opportunity to show the world what we're capable of.

5. Fear of Judgment and Criticism:

Honestly, one of thc biggest obstacles we face is the fear of being judged by others. It's like we're scared of what people will say if we step out of our comfort zone and do something different. We don't want to be labelled as too ambitious or criticized for going against the norm. But deep inside, we understand the need to overcome this barrier and stay true to who we really are. We know that we are meant for more

6. Self-Doubt and Lack of Confidence:

In moments of self-doubt, we often question our own abilities and wonder if we are truly worthy. It's like we become our own harshest critics, doubting our potential. But deep within, we yearn for something more. We need to believe in ourselves wholeheartedly and find the courage to make bold decisions that shape our lives. It's a journey, one that requires building our self-belief brick by brick.

You know, there are times when we hesitate to ask for what we truly desire. It's as if our needs, dreams, and aspirations are met with scepticism. Why should our heartfelt desires be questioned? It feels like a heavy blow, dampening our spirit and diminishing our sense of self-worth. It restricts our growth, hinders our progress, and stabs at our very self-respect. Doesn't it hurt?

But here's what I propose, my dear ladies: take a moment with me. **Place your hand over your heart and reflect.** Ask yourself, "Am I not equally responsible for the situation I find myself in? Is there anything I could have done differently to create a win-win situation for everyone involved?" Let your emotions guide you as you seek understanding and strive for a better future.

Manifesting Dreams

The Top 7 Desires of Growth-Minded Home Makers

Your identity as a homemaker extends far beyond your roles. Embrace your passions and talents, and let them define you.

As the sun dipped below the horizon, casting a warm glow over the bustling street, I walked into a charming bakery one evening, lured by the irresistible smell of freshly baked goodies. Amongst the sweet delights, I spotted a woman named Asma, a mother of two and a passionate home baker. With flour dusting her apron and a smile lighting up her eyes, she looked like a picture of contentment, but something about her demeanour told a different story.

As I approached her, she greeted me with a warm smile, but beneath it, I sensed an undercurrent of emotions waiting to break free. Those sparkling eyes held unshed tears. We struck up a conversation, and as we delved deeper, she confided in me about her inner struggles and desires.

Asma had devoted herself to her family, and while she loved being a homemaker and a mother, she couldn't help but feel a pang of dissatisfaction. Despite her tireless efforts in baking and managing the household, she felt unworthy, unappreciated, and unacknowledged. She longed for a sense of identity beyond her roles as a wife and mother.

Her self-esteem had taken a hit over the years, and she found herself dependent on her husband even for the smallest of needs. She yearned for the freedom to make her own decisions and carve a path that defined her as an individual, not just as someone's wife or mother.

Tears welled up in her eyes as she expressed her frustrations, anger, and the overwhelming feeling of being lost. It was as if her dreams were trapped within her, and she needed someone to help unlock them.

Listening to her heartfelt words, I knew that Asma was not alone in her desires. Many growth-minded homemakers faced similar struggles. With a reassuring smile, I took her hand and promised to help her discover the top seven desires that could set her on a path of self-discovery and empowerment. She wanted purpose and direction in her life, a path where she could blossom and make her dreams come true.

Let's discover the top seven desires of growth-minded homemakers like Asma. For helping you understand it better, I will use Asma as an example of issues she faced and the answers she was looking for

1. A Sense of Identity: Asma craved an identity that was uniquely hers, beyond her roles in her family. She wanted to be known for her passions and talents.

2. Appreciation and Acknowledgment: Feeling unappreciated, she desired recognition for her efforts and the work she put into her baking and home management.

3. Independence: Asma yearned for the freedom to make her own decisions, both big and small, without feeling dependent on others.

4. Fearlessness: She wanted to overcome her fears and insecurities, standing strong in the face of societal norms and expectations.

5. Self-Esteem: Asma wished to rebuild her self-esteem and embrace her worthiness as an individual.

6. Confidence: She longed to be confident in her abilities and choices, knowing that she was capable of achieving her dreams.

7. Purpose and Direction: Above all, Asma sought a path that gave her purpose and direction in life, where her aspirations could bloom.

After our heartfelt discussion, Asma made a powerful decision. She refused to let life pass her by while waiting on the sidelines. With a newfound determination, she committed to working on herself and taking charge of her own destiny.

Deeply inspired by her courage, I pledged to be her guiding companion on this transformative journey. Together, we would unlock her true potential, ignite her growth, and embark on a path of self-discovery and empowerment.

Asma's story was just the beginning, and through her desires, I knew that countless other growth-minded homemakers longed for the same transformation.

And thus, our journey commenced—an empowering quest filled with self-confidence and fulfilment. Asma's aspirations served as the catalyst for this chapter, reflecting the shared dreams of numerous growth-minded homemakers.

United, we would venture into the depths of each desire, uncovering actionable strategies to manifest them in tangible ways. Embracing the core of personal identity, we would guide individuals to embrace their innate qualities and talents. Every achievement, no matter how small, would be celebrated, nurturing a supportive environment of appreciation and recognition.

Independence would no longer be a distant dream but a tangible goal. We would uncover strategies for making confident decisions and breaking free from the limitations imposed by others. Fear would be faced head-on, empowering individuals to step out of their comfort zones and embrace their full potential.

Self-esteem would be rebuilt through self-care, self-love, and a deep understanding of personal worth. Confidence would flourish as individuals recognized their own capabilities and learned to trust their instincts. Together, we would navigate the winding paths of life, always guided by a clear sense of purpose and direction.

As I continued my journey with Asma and others like her, I couldn't help but feel grateful for the opportunity to support these growth-minded homemakers. Their desires were the seeds of transformation, and with dedication, perseverance, and a dash of creativity, we would cultivate a life of empowerment and fulfilment.

So, my fellow growth-minded homemakers, let us embark on this incredible journey together. Let us embrace our desires, step into our power, and create lives filled with purpose, joy, and the freedom to be our authentic selves. The path ahead may have its challenges, but with determination and a supportive community, we will overcome any obstacles that come our way.

With anticipation building in the air, I felt a surge of excitement as I envisioned the chapters that lay ahead. They promised a journey of exploration, personal growth, and boundless opportunities.

Now, the question arises: Are you prepared to embark on this transformative path with us? Together, we will navigate uncharted territories, unlock hidden potentials, and embrace a life of limitless possibilities. So, are you ready to take the leap and embark on this exhilarating adventure? Let's make it happen!

WINGS OF TRANSFORMATION

Empowering Yourself for Personal Growth and Independence

Taking ownership of your life is not just a choice; it's a powerful declaration of self-empowerment."

My dear Change-Makers are you ready to embark on an exciting journey of personal growth and independence? Get ready to unleash your potential and transform your life as we dive into the incredible world of self-discovery and empowerment. In this chapter, we will explore three fundamental aspects that will empower you to build your identity, assert your authority, be fearless, and confidently make your own decisions. Together, we'll cultivate self-awareness, develop a growth mindset by using the transformative power of words, and take ownership of our lives. Get ready to unlock your true potential and embrace the incredible journey ahead!

First things first, let's talk about self-awareness. It's all about getting to know yourself on a deeper level—your strengths, weaknesses, values, and aspirations. By taking the time to reflect and understand who you truly are, you gain clarity on what you want out of life. This self-awareness becomes your compass, guiding you to make choices that align with your authentic self. Knowing yourself better allows you to identify areas for growth, leverage your strengths, and make decisions that lead to personal and professional development. For that I have a small exercise that will serve as a starting point for cultivating self-awareness, leading to personal growth and improved decision-making in various aspects of homemaking.

Self-Awareness Assessment

Instructions: Take a few moments to reflect on the following questions and rate yourself on a scale of 1 to 5, with 1 being "Not at all" and 5 being "Very much." Be honest with yourself and answer based on your current level of self-awareness.

1. How well do you understand your strengths, talents, and areas for improvement?

- 1: Not at all
- 2: Somewhat
- 3: Moderately
- 4: Quite well
- 5: Very much

2. How aware are you of your emotions and how they influence your thoughts and actions?

- 1: Not at all
- 2: Somewhat

- 3: Moderately
- 4: Quite well
- 5: Very much

3. How often do you take time for self-reflection and introspection?
   - 1: Rarely or never
   - 2: Occasionally
   - 3: Sometimes
   - 4: Frequently
   - 5: Regularly

4. How open are you to receiving feedback and constructive criticism?
   - 1: Not at all
   - 2: Somewhat
   - 3: Moderately
   - 4: Quite well
   - 5: Very much

5. How well do you understand your values, beliefs, and what truly matters to you?
   - 1: Not at all
   - 2: Somewhat
   - 3: Moderately

- 4: Quite well

- 5: Very much

6. How aware are you of your personal boundaries and limits?

   - 1: Not at all

   - 2: Somewhat

   - 3: Moderately

   - 4: Quite well

   - 5: Very much

7. How in tune are you with your physical and mental well-being?

   - 1: Not at all

   - 2: Somewhat

   - 3: Moderately

   - 4: Quite well

   - 5: Very much

8. How often do you seek feedback from others to gain different perspectives?

   - 1: Rarely or never

   - 2: Occasionally

   - 3: Sometimes

   - 4: Frequently

- 5: Regularly

9. How aware are you of your communication style and how it affects your interactions with others?

- 1: Not at all
- 2: Somewhat
- 3: Moderately
- 4: Quite well
- 5: Very much

10. How willing are you to challenge your own beliefs and embrace personal growth?

- 1: Not at all
- 2: Somewhat
- 3: Moderately
- 4: Quite well
- 5: Very much

Interpreting your score:

- 10-20: You have room for improvement in cultivating self-awareness. Consider exploring self-reflection practices and seeking feedback to deepen your understanding of yourself.

- 21-30: You have a basic level of self-awareness, but there is still room to develop a deeper understanding of your thoughts, emotions, and behaviours.

- 31-40: You have a moderate level of self-awareness. Continue practicing self-reflection and seeking feedback to further enhance your self-awareness skills.

- 41-50: You have a good level of self-awareness. As you continue to nurture your self-awareness, you'll uncover hidden potentials, understand your motivations better, and cultivate a stronger sense of self. Remember, the more self-awareness you develop, the more empowered you become in navigating your life's path with clarity and purpose. Keep up the great work on your journey of personal growth and self-discovery!

The Power of Words: Cultivating a Growth Mindset

Words possess incredible transformative power, shaping our mindset and influencing how we perceive ourselves and the world. By embracing a growth mindset, we recognize that our abilities and intelligence can be developed through effort and learning. Challenges and setbacks no longer define us; instead, they become stepping stones toward our goals.

So, let's harness the power of words to cultivate a growth mindset. Replace self-limiting phrases like "I can't do it" with empowering statements such as "I'm working on it" or "I can learn and improve." When faced with setbacks, shift your perspective from "I failed" to "I experienced a setback, but I'm determined to find a solution and grow from it."

Moreover, the way we communicate with ourselves and others matters. Choose words that convey optimism, possibility, and determination. Embrace phrases like "I can overcome this," "I believe in my abilities," and "I am capable of achieving great things." These affirmations nurture resilience and foster an open mindset.

By consciously selecting uplifting words and reframing our thoughts, we unlock a world of potential. Here are three practical examples:

1. Instead of saying, "I'm not good at this," say, "I have room for growth, and with practice, I can improve."

2. Replace "I'll never be as talented as others" with "I have unique strengths, and I can develop new skills through dedication and perseverance."

3. Rather than saying, "This challenge is too difficult," reframe it as "This challenge is an opportunity for me to stretch my abilities and learn something new."

Remember, the power of words lies not only in positive affirmations but also in aligning our thoughts with an optimistic and growth-oriented outlook. Through mindful language, we shape our thoughts, beliefs, and actions, unlocking our true potential to fearlessly pursue our passions and achieve personal growth.

So, let's harness the power of our words, choose them wisely, and watch as they transform challenges into opportunities, nurture resilience, and propel us toward a fulfilling and limitless life of growth and achievement.

Taking Ownership- Charting your own course

Now, let's talk about taking ownership of your life. It's time to grab the reins and steer your life in the direction you want. When you take ownership, you acknowledge that you have the power to shape your circumstances. You make choices that reflect your values, dreams, and aspirations. No more waiting for others to dictate your path! By taking ownership, you break free from limitations, confidently navigate life's twists and turns, and build a life that's truly yours. Let me share 10 reasons why taking ownership of your life is crucial for you.

1. Personal Fulfilment: Taking ownership of your life brings joy and fulfilment as you shape your circumstances and make choices aligned with your values and aspirations.

2. Empowerment: It helps you to be the driver of your life, making decisions and pursuing your goals without relying on others.

3. Authenticity: By embracing authenticity, you break free from the need to please others and prioritize their happiness. Instead, you focus on expressing your true self and making choices that align with your core identity.

4. Growth and Development: Ownership opens doors for personal growth, learning, and skill development as you actively seek opportunities for self-improvement.

5. Overcoming Limitations: Taking ownership breaks free from limitations and empowers you to find solutions, overcome obstacles, and embrace resilience.

6. Increased Confidence: As you invest in your confidence, you'll see it expand, enabling you to embrace challenges, pursue your goals, and seize new opportunities. The journey may demand dedication, but the transformation is undeniably worth it.

7. Personal Responsibility: Your actions have consequences, and you bear full responsibility for them. Embrace this truth without blaming others or fixating on past failures. Instead, adopt a solution-focused mindset, prioritizing learning and personal growth. Own your choices, take proactive steps, and shape a better future.

8. Improved Relationships: Ownership enhances relationships by bringing authenticity, fulfilment, and healthier connections with others.

9. Resilience and Adaptability: Taking ownership equips you with resilience and adaptability skills to navigate challenges and bounce back stronger.

10. Legacy and Impact: When you take ownership of your life, you have the incredible opportunity to leave a lasting legacy and make a positive impact. Live a life that truly reflects who you are, and let your actions and choices inspire others. Be the person you aspire to be, and create a world that's better because of you.

So, my fellow growth-minded change makers, by empowering yourself for personal growth and independence, you unlock endless possibilities. You gain the confidence to explore your passions, make choices that resonate with your authentic self, and fearlessly chase your dreams. It's all about building a strong sense of identity, asserting your authority in what you do, and making decisions that shape your life on your own terms.

Communication Skills for Thriving Relationships

Cultivating Meaningful Relationships and Connections

"Balancing personal aspirations and family responsibilities requires the delicate art of open communication."

As Caring nurturers, we know how important it is to build strong bonds and nurture connections with our loved ones and peers. In this chapter, we'll explore the power of active listening, building trust, open and empathetic communication, and integrating personal aspirations with family responsibilities. So, let's embark on this journey together and discover practical solutions to enhance our relationships. Let's look at each step one by one

"*Communication is the currency of connection.*" Effective communication forms the foundation of meaningful relationships. Let's explore how we can improve our communication skills.

Step I: Active Listening

"Listening with the heart creates bridges of understanding."

Imagine this: You're having a chat with a close friend who seems upset. Instead of waiting for your turn to speak, focus on giving them your full attention. Make eye contact, show genuine interest, and ask questions that encourage them to share their thoughts and feelings. This active listening approach creates a safe space for them to open up, knowing that their words truly matter. By practicing active listening, we forge authentic connections and show others that we genuinely care without giving any opinions or advice.

Step II: Empathy and Compassion -

Take the time to understand others' perspectives by putting yourself in their shoes. Seek to comprehend their experiences, emotions, and challenges. Empathy strengthens bonds and promotes understanding.

Step III: Managing emotions

It is crucial for homemakers who aim to build authority and independence to learn how to manage their emotions. It begins with cultivating self-awareness, understanding our own emotions, strengths, and growth areas. Take time to reflect on your feelings and triggers, and practice recognizing and labelling your emotions.

Next, focus on regulating your emotions by developing healthy coping mechanisms. Engage in activities like deep breathing exercises, mindfulness, or journaling to calm yourself during moments of stress or overwhelm. Find healthy outlets for emotions, such as talking to a trusted friend or engaging in creative pursuits.

It is highly advised to prioritize activities that bring you joy and relaxation, whether it's taking a walk in nature, practicing hobbies, or spending quality time with loved ones. Taking care of yourself physically, mentally, and emotionally will equip you to navigate challenges with resilience and a positive mindset.

Step IV: Building Trust:

"Trust =The Foundation of Meaningful Relationships"

Trust is like the glue that holds relationships together. It relies on reliability, honesty, and keeping our promises. Let's say you promised your partner that you'd help them with a task. By following through on your commitment, you demonstrate that you can be trusted. And when trust is broken, it's important to address it openly and work on rebuilding it. Trust creates a safe and supportive environment where personal growth and empowerment can thrive. There is nothing more motivating and powerful than the trust your loved one places in you!

Step V: Integrating Personal Aspirations and Family Responsibilities

As growth-minded homemakers, we often juggle personal aspirations and family responsibilities. It can be challenging, however, it's possible to find a balance. When you have a dream or goal, share it with your loved ones and seek their support and understanding. Find common ground where personal growth and family values can coexist harmoniously. You have succeeded in your art of communication, only when both parties arrive at a win-win solution. If they win and you lose, it will make you angry and frustrated. If you win and they lose, you will end up feeling guilty and miserable.

Step VI: Prioritize Open and Empathetic Communication with your spouse

Imagine you're sitting down with your spouse after a long day. They seem preoccupied. Instead of assuming things or brushing it off, actively listen and ask them about their day. You sense something might be bothering them, even if they haven't shared it explicitly. Create a safe and open space for them to express themselves, showing empathy and understanding.

Listen patiently to their concerns, allowing them to share their thoughts and emotions without judgment. Instead of jumping in with immediate solutions, validate their feelings and let them know you're there for them. This open and empathetic communication builds a stronger connection, fostering trust and mutual support.

Open and empathetic communication transcends mere problem-solving conversations. It encompasses a profound understanding of your partner's aspirations, desires, and needs. Equally essential is the art of timely expression, employing language that not only captures their attention but also invites their active engagement in finding solutions.

Here are a few practical examples to get you thinking:

1. Create dedicated quality time with your spouse: Set aside specific moments where both of you agree to put away distractions, including mobile phones. It could be during meals, walks, or bedtime routines. Use this time to engage in meaningful conversation and deepen your connection.

2. Express your feelings: Share how their preoccupation with their mobile phone makes you feel. Use "I" statements to communicate your emotions without blaming or criticizing. For instance, say something like, "I miss our uninterrupted conversations and would love to reconnect without distractions."

3. Plan activities together: Engage in shared activities that require active participation. Go for an outing, take up a hobby, or cook a small meal together. These shared experiences provide opportunities for communication and bonding.

4. Set boundaries: Establish specific zones or times in your home where mobile phone use is limited or discouraged. For example, designate the bedroom as a device-free zone to promote uninterrupted connection and relaxation.

5. Lead by example: Demonstrate the importance of being present and engaged by practicing it yourself. When you spend time together, put your own phone away and focus on the conversation. Your partner will notice your attentiveness and be more likely to follow suit.

Remember, approach the situation with understanding and empathy. Express your desire for deeper connection and quality time. By addressing the issue in a gentle and respectful manner, you can work together to prioritize open and empathetic communication, fostering a stronger bond in your relationship.

Cultivating meaningful relationships and connections is an incredible journey that enriches our lives. By actively listening, building trust, practicing open and empathetic communication, and integrating personal aspirations with family responsibilities, we nurture deep connections that fuel our personal growth and empower us on our path. Remember, it takes effort and commitment, but the rewards are truly worth it. So, let's take these lessons to heart and create a nurturing environment where your relationships thrive.

Key Takeaways:

1. Active listening involves being fully present and understanding the other person's perspective.

2. Trust is built on reliability, honesty, and keeping our commitments.

3. Open and empathetic communication creates a space where people feel heard and valued.

4. Integrating personal aspirations with family responsibilities requires open communication and finding common ground.

5. By managing your emotions and honing your communication skills, you can foster stronger relationships These valuable traits will empower you to navigate the intricacies of personal connections with grace and resilience.

Action Points to Implement

1. Practice active listening by giving your full attention, maintaining eye contact, and asking open-ended questions.

2. Practice communication techniques and work on your emotions

3. Prioritize quality time with your loved ones to create opportunities for open and empathetic communication.

4. Communicate your personal aspirations to your family and seek their support and understanding.

5. Find a balance between pursuing your individual goals and fulfilling your family responsibilities by finding common ground and supporting each other's aspirations.

Designing a Blueprint for Balance and Fulfilment

Prioritizing Well-being and Finding Balance in Your Life

"In the whirlwind of modern life, finding balance is not a luxury but a necessity."

Life can be a whirlwind of responsibilities, expectations, and constant demands, but fear not! In this chapter, we'll explore how you can take charge of your well-being, build resilience, and create a life that aligns with your values and brings you joy. So, let's dive right in and embark on this journey toward a more balanced and fulfilling life.

I. Understanding Well-being:

When we talk about well-being, we're talking about taking care of yourself in all aspects—physically, mentally, emotionally, and socially. It's about finding harmony and fulfilment in each of these dimensions. Think of it as a puzzle with different pieces coming together to create a beautiful picture of overall well-being. By nurturing each dimension, you're setting the foundation for a happier and healthier life.

II. The Challenges of Modern Life:

Let's face it—modern life comes with its fair share of challenges. We often find ourselves juggling multiple roles, dealing with stress, and succumbing to societal pressures. But here's the secret: You have the power to overcome these challenges and find balance. It starts with recognizing the areas that are causing imbalance and taking intentional actions to counteract them.

III. Prioritizing Self-Care:

Self-care is not just a buzzword—it's a vital component of well-being. It's about making yourself a priority and ensuring your needs are met. Self-care looks different for everyone. It could be as simple as taking a long bath, going for a walk-in nature, or indulging in a hobby you love. Remember, self-care is not selfish—it's necessary for your well-being.

IV. Setting Boundaries:

Boundaries act as your personal guardrails, protecting your time, energy, and emotions. By setting boundaries, you're creating a safe space where you can thrive. It's about learning to say "no" when something doesn't align with your well-being and "yes" to things that bring you joy and fulfillment. Setting boundaries empowers you to take control of your life and make decisions that are in line with your values. We will be talking more about this in our next chapter.

V. Nurturing a Development Mindset

Nurturing a development mindset involves fostering a belief in your capacity to learn, grow, and improve through dedication and effort. By embracing this mindset, you can overcome fear, self-doubt, and limiting beliefs. It encourages you to step outside of your comfort zone, take ownership of your decisions, and embrace new opportunities for personal and professional growth. However, several common mistakes can hinder the development of this mindset. Let's explore a few of these mistakes and their corresponding solutions:

Mistake: Seeking perfection and fearing failure.

Solution: Embrace the idea that failure is a natural part of the learning process. Shift your focus from perfection to progress, and view failures as opportunities for growth and improvement.

Mistake: Comparing yourself to others and feeling inadequate.

Solution: Recognize that everyone has their own unique journey and strengths. Focus on your own progress and celebrate your achievements, rather than comparing yourself to others.

Mistake: Overloading yourself with too many goals or tasks.

Solution: Prioritize your goals and focus on a few key areas for growth. Break them down into smaller, achievable steps to maintain momentum and avoid overwhelm.

Mistake: Not seeking continuous learning opportunities.

Solution: Cultivate a thirst for knowledge and actively seek opportunities for growth. Attend workshops, read books, take courses, and engage in conversations that expand your knowledge and skills. Education is not a one-time process that's limited to schools and colleges. So why stop learning once it's over?

VI. Creating a Well-being Routine:

A well-being routine is like a roadmap that guides you toward balance and fulfillment. It's about intentionally incorporating activities that nourish your mind, body, and soul. Whether it's practicing yoga, journaling, or spending quality time with loved ones, creating a routine that supports your well-being is essential. Find what activities bring you joy and make them a non-negotiable part of your daily or weekly schedule.

Key Takeaways:

1. Prioritize all aspects of your well-being—physical, mental, emotional, and social.

2. Set boundaries to protect your time, energy, and emotions.

3. Cultivate a growth mindset to overcome challenges and embrace personal growth.

4. Create a well-being routine that incorporates activities you enjoy and that nurture your mind, body, and soul.

5. Remember, self-care is not selfish—it's necessary for your overall well-being.

Action Points to Implement:

1. Assess your well-being in each dimension—physical, mental, emotional, and social—and identify areas that need attention.

2. Practice setting boundaries by saying "no" to one activity or commitment that doesn't align with your well-being.

3. Embrace a growth mindset by challenging a negative belief and taking a small step outside of your comfort zone.

4. Designate specific times in your schedule for self-care activities that bring you joy and nourish your well-being.

5. Make a commitment to read at least one educational or inspiring book every month and actively apply the knowledge gained from it to your personal and professional life.

FINDING YOUR VOICE

Setting Boundaries - Empowering Yourself and Nurturing Well-being

"Setting boundaries liberates you from the weight of others' expectations."

Get ready to dive into a very important chapter, know everything about setting boundaries, an empowering skill that can transform your life. In this fast-paced world, it's easy to get overwhelmed and lose sight of your own needs. But not to worry, because I'm here to guide you through the process of setting boundaries, reclaiming your power, and nurturing your well-being.

Understanding Boundaries:

Picture this: boundaries are like your personal shield, protecting your time, energy, and emotional well-being. They're like the fences around your beautiful garden, keeping out anything that doesn't belong and allowing the things that nourish you to thrive. Setting boundaries means defining your limits and communicating them to others. It's all about creating a life that truly reflects who you are and what you need to flourish.

Let me tell you the story of Radhika to help you understand better. Radhika, a warm-hearted 35-year-old woman, found joy in taking care of her family. Her loved ones cherished her, but she had a hard time saying no when asked to do tasks. Whether it was her in-laws, neighbours, or friends, Radhika would always say yes, even if it took a toll on her health.

The endless household chores and commitments left Radhika frustrated and exhausted. Despite completing the work, she would find herself apologizing. Her friends took her efforts for granted, assuming she would always be there to help. They would say things like, "Radhika will do it; she won't say no" or "Why ask Radhika for her opinion? She'll do whatever we say."

This started to hurt Radhika's self-esteem, and her personal relationships began to suffer. She was a talented woman who had completed an interior design course but had set aside her ambitions to focus on her home. When she came to me, she was aware of the impact her decisions had on her well-being. She was worried that her constant state of frustration and inability to speak up for herself would turn her into a bitter person, and she desperately wanted to avoid that.

"Farida, I am really scared of losing myself," she confided in me. That's when I provided her with the solutions that can help you if you're facing similar challenges. The following steps will guide you in finding solutions to the issues you face.

Recognize Your Worth: Setting boundaries starts with recognizing the inherent value within you. Embrace the belief that you deserve to have your needs met and your boundaries respected. Let go of any self-doubt or limiting beliefs that try to diminish your worth. You are deserving of a life that honours your true essence.

As we continued our journey together, I constantly reminded Radhika of her worth. I encouraged her to reflect on her unique qualities and the contributions she made to her family and loved ones. By understanding her value, Radhika gained the strength to say no when it did not sit well with her without feeling guilty of offending anyone.

It wasn't an easy process, as she had to confront her own self-doubt and overcome the beliefs that had held her back for so long. But with each step, Radhika embraced her worthiness more firmly. She realized that her needs and well-being were just as important as anyone else's.

Radhika let go of the self-sacrificing mindset that had once defined her. She no longer allowed others to take advantage of her kindness and willingness to help. Instead, she held her head high, knowing that she deserved to be treated with respect and consideration.

This shift in mindset brought about remarkable changes in Radhika's life. She experienced a newfound sense of confidence and empowerment. As she set boundaries and said no when necessary, she regained control over her time and energy. Radhika found a balance between meeting her own needs and caring for her loved ones, without compromising her own well-being.

The transformation was visible in her relationships as well. Radhika's loved ones began to appreciate her boundaries and respected her decisions. They realized that her saying no didn't diminish her love for them but rather allowed her to show up in a more authentic and present way.

Establishing Personal Boundaries:

Now it's time to roll up your sleeves and establish your personal boundaries. Start by reflecting on your values, priorities, and what truly matters to you. What activities or behaviours make you feel drained or overwhelmed? Identify those areas where you need to set limits. Then, armed with self-assurance, communicate your boundaries clearly and assertively. Remember, it's not about being selfish—it's about honouring your needs while respecting others.

Here are a few Questions to help you set Boundaries

1) *Defining Your Boundaries*: What behaviours or actions that you feel cross your personal boundaries and negatively impact your well-being?

2) *Expressing Your Boundaries*: How you can express your boundaries in a firm yet respectful manner, ensuring that others understand your expectations and don't feel disrespected?

3) *Empowering Expressions*: What assertive statements or phrases can you use to communicate your boundaries confidently and respectfully? (Example: "I have made plans for the weekend and won't be able to accommodate any last-minute changes." "I have committed to other obligations, so I won't be able to attend the event. Thank you for understanding.")

Maintaining Boundaries in Relationships:

Boundaries aren't just for your own benefit; they're also essential for maintaining healthy relationships to promote respect, trust, and open communication. However, it's important to acknowledge that setting boundaries may sometimes face resistance or pushback from others. Stay strong and develop strategies for handling conflicts or disagreements that may arise. Remember, healthy relationships are built on mutual understanding and respect for each other's space.

Implementing Boundaries in Different Areas of Life

Boundaries aren't limited to specific areas of your life—they're meant to be integrated into every aspect. Learn how to set boundaries at work, such as defining your workload, managing your time effectively, and communicating your availability.

Don't forget about setting boundaries with yourself. Practice self-discipline, honour your limits, and prioritize self-care to maintain a healthy balance.

By valuing yourself, communicating assertively, and maintaining healthy relationships, you are creating a life that honours your well-being and empowers you to thrive. Remember, setting boundaries is a continuous process that requires self-awareness, self-compassion, and practice. Embrace the power of boundaries, and watch as they uplift and transform your life

Key Takeaways:

1. Boundaries are your personal shield, protecting your well-being and allowing you to flourish.

2. Embrace your self-worth and believe that you deserve to have your boundaries respected.

3. Reflect on your values and needs to establish boundaries that align with your authentic self.

4. Maintain healthy relationships by communicating your boundaries assertively and addressing resistance.

5. Extend boundary-setting skills to all areas of your life, including work, personal relationships, and self-care.

Action Points to Implement:

1. Reflect on your values and needs and identify one area of your life where you need to establish a boundary.

2. Practice assertive communication by role-playing or scripting conversations where you express your boundaries clearly and respectfully.

3. Implement a boundary-setting technique, such as using "I" statements or setting time limits for specific activities.

4. Seek support from loved ones or a therapist to navigate challenges or resistance you may face when establishing boundaries.

5. Regularly assess and adjust your boundaries as needed, ensuring they align with your evolving needs and values.

FROM OVERWHELM TO SUCCESS

Setting the Stage for Success: The Key Principles of Effective Goal Setting

---

"Within the symphony of life, where chaos dances and time weaves its intricate melodies, goal setting emerges as the guiding light. It illuminates our path, infusing intention into each note, and harmonizes the rhythms of our existence."

We all have dreams and aspirations that reside within us, waiting to be awakened and brought to life. However, I have observed that sometimes these dreams lay dormant, especially among the incredible individuals who dedicate their lives to being homemakers. In this chapter, I want to ignite the spark of possibility within you, inspiring you to dream boldly and without limits. Together, we will explore a simple yet powerful goal-setting technique that has empowered countless individuals, including homemakers, to maximize their productivity, create balance, and achieve their dreams

Understanding the Importance of Goal Setting:

As an experienced coach guiding individuals on their journey to success, I have witnessed the transformative power of effective goal-setting. In this chapter, we embark on a remarkable exploration together, uncovering a simple yet profound technique that has brought immense clarity and focus to my client's lives.

Before we embark on this transformative journey, I invite you to grab a pen and paper and fully immerse yourself in this chapter. Let go of any distractions and embrace this opportunity to give your undivided attention to the process that lies ahead.

Drawing upon my expertise as a graphologist, I offer a unique perspective on the connection between goal setting and brain function. Our intricate minds generate a multitude of thoughts, approximately 60,000 in a single day. Amidst this flurry of mental activity, writing our goals down becomes a powerful signal to our brain, affirming the importance and priority we assign to them.

Aligning with Purpose: Write down at least 100 innermost desires that you have. Allow your imagination to roam freely, unburdened by limitations or doubts. Allow yourself to dream, to aspire, those dreams that seem out of reach. As you bring your aspirations to life on paper, you will witness the emergence of a tapestry woven with the threads of your deepest yearnings. Each desire represents a step closer to the life you envision, and within these aspirations lie the seeds of your future success.

With your comprehensive list of 100 goals in hand, let us embark on the transformative process of selection. Deliberate upon each goal, allowing your intuition to guide you. Choose 10 goals that ignite a spark within you, that align with your values and passions, and that hold the potential to unlock your greatest potential.

As you curate this refined collection of goals, allow yourself to bask in the exhilaration of possibility. These 10 chosen goals stand as beacons of hope, representing the profound impact you are capable of making in your own life.

Now, dear ambitious designers, it is time to unveil the crown jewels of your aspirations. From the carefully selected 10 goals, identify the top 3 that resonate most deeply with your soul. These cherished goals become the focal points of your journey, the driving force that propels you forward with unwavering determination.

Focus your energy, time, and resources on these top 3 goals, committing yourself wholeheartedly to their realization. Let them guide your actions, inform your decisions, and infuse your daily life with purpose. As you make progress and witness the fruits of your labour, celebrate these milestones, for they mark the culmination of your unwavering dedication and unwavering commitment.

Upon reaching each milestone, take a moment to honour your achievements, then embrace the next set of goals from your initial list of 10. By repeating this process, you create a symphony of continuous growth, propelling yourself towards an extraordinary existence.

As your trusted coach, I encourage you to view this goal-setting journey as a lifelong practice. Regularly review and reassess your goals, allowing them to evolve alongside your own personal growth. Remain open to new aspirations that may arise, for they hold the potential to enrich your journey even further.

I am sharing my invaluable insights and transformative techniques with you. All you need to do is work on this worksheet. This is so important that I am giving this worksheet example here in the book and a link for those who wish to take the printouts too.

Goal Getting Worksheet

Brainstorm: Take a moment to write down at least 100 goals that resonate with your aspirations and desires. Let your imagination flow freely and don't worry about limitations or feasibility at this stage.

Goal Selection: From your extensive list, carefully choose 10 goals that hold the most meaning and align with your values and passions. These goals should inspire and motivate you on your journey.

Top 3 Goals: Now, identify the top 3 goals from your selected list of 10. These are the goals that resonate most deeply with your soul and represent your core priorities which you will be working on for the next 1 year.

Goal 1:

Why is this goal important to you?

How will achieving this goal impact your life positively?

Goal 2:

Why is this goal important to you?

How will achieving this goal impact your life positively?

Goal 3:

Why is this goal important to you?

How will achieving this goal impact your life positively?

Action Plan: For each of your top 3 goals, outline specific actions and steps you can take to work towards their achievement. Break down each goal into manageable tasks and set target dates for completion.

Goal 1:

Action Steps:

1--

2 --

3 --

Target Dates:

Task 1:

Task 2:

Task 3:

Goal 2:

Action Steps:

1--

2 --

3 --

Target Dates:

Task 1:

Task 2:

Task 3:

Goal 3:

Action Steps:

1--

2 --

3 --

Target Dates:

Task 1:

Task 2:

Task 3:

Review and Celebrate: Regularly review your progress towards your goals and make adjustments as necessary. A weekly review works wonders. Celebrate each milestone you achieve along the way, acknowledging the progress you are making towards your desired outcomes.

By following this worksheet and consistently working on your goals, you will pave the way for personal growth, fulfillment, and success. Remember, this is a journey of self-discovery and continuous improvement. Embrace the process, stay committed, and celebrate each step forward.

Overcoming Challenges in Goal Setting and Time Management:

Goal setting and time management come with their fair share of challenges. Procrastination, distractions, and time-wasting activities can derail your progress. Combat these challenges by breaking tasks into smaller chunks, setting deadlines, and eliminating unnecessary distractions. One simple technique I use is having a timer and focusing only on activity for the next 2 hours. That way a lot of work gets done and you get a feeling of accomplishment on completing something substantial. All you need is a mobile phone and set a timer to it. Get -Set -Go....

Key Takeaways:

1. Setting clear goals gives you direction and purpose in managing your time effectively.

2. Involve others in your goal-setting process for valuable input and support.

3. Prioritize tasks by setting boundaries and focusing on what truly matters to you.

4. Connect your goals with your emotions and values for greater motivation.

5. Break big goals into smaller, actionable steps and celebrate each milestone along the way.

Action Points to Implement:

1. Identify 3 goal that aligns with your passions and values, and break it down into smaller, manageable tasks.

2. Share your goal with someone you trust and ask for their input and support.

3. Set boundaries by eliminating one non-essential task or distraction from your daily routine.

4. Schedule dedicated time for goal-related activities in your calendar and treat them as non-negotiable appointments.

5. Regularly review your progress, make adjustments as needed, and celebrate your achievements along the way.

SCAN ME

THE WELLNESS CODE

Transforming Your Health from the Inside Out

"Balance is not something you find, it's something you create."

Picture this: a life filled with balance, productivity, and joy. Sounds amazing, right? Well, get ready to make it a reality!

Changes in a Woman's Body:

Women's bodies undergo various changes throughout their lives, including menstruation, pregnancy, and menopause. Each stage brings unique challenges and considerations. Menstruation involves hormonal fluctuations and may cause symptoms like cramps, mood swings, and fatigue. Pregnancy requires extra care for both the mother's and the baby's health, including proper nutrition, regular prenatal check-ups, and exercise as recommended by healthcare professionals. Menopause involves hormonal shifts that may lead to symptoms like hot flashes, mood changes, and decreased bone density.

What you need to know about every stage

Menstruation: During menstruation, hormonal fluctuations occur as part of the menstrual cycle. This can lead to symptoms like cramps, mood swings, fatigue, and bloating. 3 ways you can take care of yourself during this time:

- Practice self-care rituals like warm baths, gentle stretching, and relaxation exercises to alleviate cramps.
- Prioritize rest and sleep to combat fatigue and replenish energy.
- Consider using heating pads or over-the-counter pain relievers to manage discomfort.

Pregnancy: Pregnancy brings significant changes to a woman's body to support the growth and development of the baby. It requires extra care and attention. Here are 3 ways you can take care of yourself during pregnancy:

- Attend regular prenatal check-ups to monitor the health of both the mother and the baby.
- Get sufficient rest and sleep to support your body's needs during this transformative time.
- Seek emotional support from loved ones or join support groups to share experiences and manage any anxieties or concerns.

Menopause: Menopause marks the end of a woman's reproductive years and involves hormonal shifts. Common symptoms include hot flashes, mood changes, and decreased bone density. Here are five ways to take care of yourself during menopause:

- Wear light clothing and use fans or cooling techniques to manage hot flashes.
- Practice stress-reduction techniques like deep breathing exercises, meditation, or gentle yoga to support emotional well-being.
- Ensure a calcium-rich diet and consider supplements to support bone health.
- Engage in regular weight-bearing exercises, such as walking or dancing, to help maintain bone density.
- Seek medical advice if symptoms are impacting your quality of life, as hormone replacement therapy or other treatments may be beneficial.

Psychosomatic Diseases and Autoimmune Diseases:

Psychosomatic diseases are physical conditions that are influenced by emotional factors. These are disease we create for ourselves. They are the unresolved issues, the anger, pain and frustration you choose to swallow and now your body is paying the price! Let me give you some examples.

Irritable Bowel Syndrome (IBS): This gastrointestinal disorder can cause abdominal pain, bloating, and changes in bowel habits. It is often associated with stress, anxiety, and emotional distress.

Migraines: Severe headaches that are often accompanied by sensitivity to light, sound, and nausea. Emotional stress, anxiety, and certain triggers can contribute to the onset of migraines.

Eczema: A skin condition characterized by itchy, inflamed patches. Emotional stress and anxiety can aggravate symptoms and trigger flare-ups.

Asthma: A chronic respiratory condition characterized by inflammation and narrowing of the airways. Emotional stress and anxiety can trigger asthma attacks in susceptible individuals.

Autoimmune diseases occur when the immune system mistakenly attacks healthy cells. Some examples include

Rheumatoid Arthritis: This autoimmune disease primarily affects the joints, causing inflammation, pain, and stiffness. It occurs when the immune system attacks the lining of the joints.

Lupus: Lupus is a systemic autoimmune disease that can affect various organs and tissues in the body. It can cause symptoms such as joint pain, skin rashes, fatigue, and organ inflammation.

Multiple Sclerosis (MS): MS is a chronic autoimmune disease that affects the central nervous system, leading to communication problems between the brain and the rest of the body. It can cause a wide range of symptoms, including fatigue, muscle weakness, coordination difficulties, and cognitive impairment.

Type 1 Diabetes: This autoimmune disease occurs when the immune system mistakenly destroys insulin-producing cells in the pancreas. It leads to high blood sugar levels and requires lifelong management with insulin therapy.

Please note: Follow recommended medical advice and treatment plans if diagnosed with an autoimmune disease, and engage in self-care practices that support your specific condition.

Understanding Women's Health: A Holistic Approach to Well-being

A healthy routine is all about nurturing yourself from the inside out. It's about creating habits that fuel your mind, body, and soul. Imagine starting your day with a refreshing workout, nourishing your body with wholesome meals, practicing mindfulness, and dedicating time for self-care activities. These healthy habits will have a profound impact on your overall well-being. Embrace them with open arms and watch as your life transforms.

1. Physical Well-being:

a) Exercise: Engage in regular physical activity to strengthen your body, improve cardiovascular health, and boost mood. Incorporate a mix of cardiovascular exercises and strength training into your routine.

b) Sleep: Prioritize quality sleep to rejuvenate your body and mind. Create a soothing bedtime routine, maintain consistent sleep and wake times, and create a sleep-friendly environment. Remember the 3R principal Sleep Power - Rest, Renewal, Rejuvenation

c) Diet: Follow a balanced and nutritious diet, focusing on whole foods, fruits, vegetables, lean proteins, and healthy fats. Consider specific nutrient needs for different life stages, such as calcium during menopause or prenatal vitamins during pregnancy.

d) Regular Health Check-ups: Schedule routine check-ups with your healthcare provider to monitor your overall health, including breast exams, Pap smears, mammograms, and other recommended screenings.

e) Hormonal Harmony: Support hormonal balance through a healthy lifestyle, stress management techniques, and seeking professional advice if needed.

2. Emotional Balance and Self-image:

a) Stress Management: Prioritize stress management techniques, such as deep breathing, meditation, mindfulness, and engaging in activities that bring you joy and relaxation.

b) Emotional Well-being: Cultivate a strong support network, practice self-care activities, and seek therapy or counseling if needed to address emotional challenges, trauma, or mental health concerns.

c) Self-image Issues: Embrace and celebrate your unique beauty. Challenge societal standards by focusing on self-acceptance, positive affirmations, and engaging in activities that boost your self-confidence.

Designing Your Ideal Routine:

Now comes the fun part–designing a routine that fits like a glove with your lifestyle and priorities. Think of it as crafting a personalized roadmap for your day. Start by considering your morning and evening rituals, work or study schedules, self-care activities, and time for relationships. Remember, Rome wasn't built in a day, so don't overwhelm yourself with drastic changes. Take it one step at a time, making small adjustments along the way.

Balancing Act: Example of a simple routine for conscious homemakers

Morning:

1. Wake up at a consistent time that allows for sufficient rest, ideally 7-8 hours of sleep.

2. Start the day with a moment of gratitude or mindfulness meditation. Take a few deep breaths, reflect on the positive aspects of your life.

3. Hydrate your body by drinking a glass of water.

4. Engage in light stretching or gentle exercise to awaken your body and promote blood circulation.

5. Enjoy a nutritious breakfast consisting of whole grains, fruits, proteins, and healthy fats.

Daytime:

1. Create a schedule or to-do list for the day, prioritizing tasks based on importance and urgency.

2. Allocate dedicated time slots for household chores, such as cleaning, cooking, and organizing.

3. Incorporate breaks throughout the day to rest, stretch, or engage in short mindfulness practice.

4. Take advantage of children's nap times or school hours to pursue personal hobbies, and skill development, or engage in activities that bring you joy and fulfillment. Remember to REST in between to rejuvenate yourselves and you don't feel drained when your children come home.

5. Prepare and enjoy nourishing meals and snacks, incorporating a variety of fresh ingredients.

Afternoon/Evening:

1. Set aside time for self-care activities that recharge your energy and well-being. This can include a warm bath, reading, practicing a hobby, or spending quality time with loved ones. Remember to REST in between to rejuvenate yourselves and you don't feel drained when your children come home.

2. Engage in light physical activity, such as going for a walk or doing yoga, to refresh your body and mind.

3. Prepare and savor a balanced dinner, emphasizing vegetables, lean proteins, and whole grains. As far as possible learn to delegate tasks, no more chopping and cutting the veggies, get your maid to do it to save you time.

4. Create an evening wind-down routine that signals your body and mind to relax. This can involve dimming lights, avoiding screens, and engaging in calming activities such as reading or listening to soothing music.

5. Aim to have a consistent bedtime routine and prioritize getting adequate sleep.

Remember, this is just a sample routine, and you can customize it based on your preferences and priorities. The key is to find a balance that allows you to fulfill your responsibilities as a homemaker while also taking care of your physical and emotional well-being. Don't try to do everything, you will exhaust yourself, the idea is to create your own routine according to your lifestyle.

Key Takeaways:

- A healthy routine has the power to enhance your overall well-being and bring balance into your life.

- Identifying your priorities allows you to align your routine with what truly matters to you.

- Start small and gradually incorporate healthy habits into your routine.

- Be flexible and resilient in the face of challenges, and seek support from your loved ones.

- Sustaining your routine requires regular evaluation, adjustment, and celebrating your progress.

Action Points to Implement:

1. Reflect on your values and aspirations to identify your priorities in life.

2. Design a daily or weekly routine that revolves around your priorities.

3. Start with one healthy habit and gradually add more over time.

4. Track your progress and celebrate small wins along the way.

5. Seek support from loved ones or join a community to stay motivated and accountable.

EMBRACING THE UNKNOWN

Overcoming Challenges and Embracing Fearlessness

"Confidence is the flame that flickers within us, casting away the shadows of doubt and illuminating the path to our limitless potential."

Life is full of ups and downs, twists and turns, and it's how we face these challenges that truly define us. In this chapter, we're going to dive deep into the world of resilience, a growth mindset, and unwavering confidence. Are you ready to conquer your fears and rise above any obstacle that comes your way?

Understanding Challenges:

Challenges, my friend, are a natural part of life's journey. They come in all shapes and sizes, testing our strength, resolve, and determination. But guess what? Challenges are not roadblocks, but opportunities for growth and self-discovery. They push us out of our comfort zones and enable us to discover our true potential.

Embracing Fearlessness:

Now, let's talk about fearlessness—the secret ingredient in overcoming challenges. Fear has a sneaky way of holding us back, whispering doubts and what-ifs in our ears. But we won't let it win, will we? No way! Embracing fearlessness means acknowledging those fears, but not letting them paralyze us. It means taking risks, stepping outside our comfort zones, and facing challenges head-on with unwavering courage.

Building Resilience:

Resilience is the key to bouncing back from challenges. It's like having a spring in your step, an unshakable belief in yourself, and the ability to rise stronger after every fall. Building resilience means developing a growth mindset—seeing setbacks as opportunities to learn and grow. It's about cultivating inner strength, practicing self-compassion, and seeking support when needed.

Strategies for Overcoming Challenges:

Now, let's get practical and explore some strategies for overcoming challenges. Develop negotiation and problem-solving skills. When faced with a challenge, take a deep breath, assess the situation, and brainstorm possible solutions. Remember, you're more resourceful than you think!

Boosting Confidence:

Confidence is your secret weapon in conquering challenges. It's like a fire within you, fuelling your determination and propelling you forward. To boost your confidence, practice positive self-talk—replace self-doubt with empowering affirmations. Visualize yourself overcoming challenges and achieving your goals. Surround yourself with supportive people who believe in you and lift you up.

Allow me to share a simple yet effective exercise I get my clients to do to help them boost their confidence level.

Power Posing:

Adopting confident body language can positively impact your mindset. Practice power poses, such as standing tall with your hands on your hips (like a superhero) or raising your arms in a victory pose. Research suggests that these poses can boost feelings of confidence and empowerment. Do it in front of the mirror. Say the sentence with full energy "FARIDA YOU ARE AMAZING, I LOVE YOU" Repeat this sentence 10-15 times daily and see the shift in your confidence level

Maintaining a Growth Mindset:

A growth mindset is a game-changer when it comes to overcoming challenges. It's about believing in your ability to learn, adapt, and grow. Embrace the power of yet–instead of saying, "I can't do it," say, "I can't do it yet."

Actively seek out learning opportunities and new experiences. Take up new hobbies, enrol in courses, attend workshops, or engage in activities that challenge you intellectually or creatively. Embrace the joy of learning and the growth that comes with it. Remember, you're constantly evolving and becoming a better version of yourself.

Embracing Fearlessness in Decision-Making:

Sometimes you have to make difficult decisions. Embrace your intuition, trust your instincts, and be confident in your choices. Remember, no decision is set in stone–life is a journey of constant course corrections.

Embrace the freedom to make decisions, learn from them, and adjust your path along the way. You are the author of your own story.

Key Takeaways

1. Challenges are opportunities for growth

2. Acknowledge your fears but don't let them paralyze you. Take risks, step out of your comfort zone, and face challenges with unwavering courage.

3. See setbacks as opportunities to learn and grow. Cultivate inner strength, practice self-compassion, and seek support when needed.

4. Develop negotiation and problem-solving skills. Assess the situation, brainstorm solutions, and tap into your resourcefulness.

5. Practice positive self-talk, visualize success, and surround yourself with supportive people who believe in you. Adopt power poses and affirmations to boost your confidence level.

Action Points:

1. Stand tall with hands on hips or adopt victory poses in front of a mirror. Repeat affirmations to make the exercise more potent.

2. Instead of saying "I can't," add "yet" to the end and believe in your ability to learn and grow.

3. Engage in new hobbies, enrol in courses, and attend workshops that challenge you intellectually or creatively.

4. Trust your instincts, be confident in your choices, and remember that decisions can be adjusted along your life's journey.

5. Develop a growth mindset, see setbacks as learning opportunities, cultivate inner strength, and seek support when facing challenges.

REWIRE YOUR MINDSET

Challenging Negative and Restrictive Beliefs

"The garden of your dreams can only flourish if you uproot the weeds of self-doubt and nurture the seeds of empowering beliefs."

Negative beliefs can be real troublemakers in our lives. They sneak in and bring everything to a screeching halt, causing all sorts of problems. Imagine you're a homemaker, trying to manage your household responsibilities and take care of your family. But these negative beliefs come along and start wreaking havoc. They make you doubt your abilities, leaving you feeling overwhelmed and incapable of tackling even the simplest tasks. They create a sense of helplessness, making it difficult for you to find joy and satisfaction in your daily routine. These beliefs limit your potential, making you miss out on exciting opportunities for personal growth and happiness. It's time to put a stop to these beliefs and break free from their grip. You deserve a life filled with confidence, progress, and unlimited possibilities.

Understanding Negative and Restrictive Beliefs:

In my practice spanning over a decade, I have had the privilege of working with remarkable and beautiful women who, despite their potential, often feel a sense of emptiness. The silence surrounding them is deafening, caused by the thoughts and ideas they hold about themselves and the world, which hinder their growth and confine them to their comfort zones. It's like being bound by invisible chains, preventing them from pursuing their dreams and taking courageous steps forward. However, here's the exciting part: once these beliefs are recognized and acknowledged, they can be challenged and conquered!

I remember coaching a talented homemaker who held a burning desire to start her own business. She had exceptional culinary skills and a genuine love for cooking, but she felt constrained by the belief that she lacked the time and resources to turn her passion into a profitable career. However, during our coaching session, a world of possibilities began to unfold before her eyes. Together, we explored numerous avenues she had never considered before. As she realized the potential and opportunities available to her, the weight of her self-imposed limitations lifted, and she felt a sense of liberation. With validation and a gentle nudge, she started to reimagine her dream, and once she did, there was no stopping her. She began making empowered choices for herself and her family, moving forward with confidence and determination. It was remarkable to witness her transformation from a hesitant dreamer to an unstoppable force, fuelled by her passion and a renewed belief in herself.

Identifying Your Negative and Restrictive Beliefs:

Now, it's time to do some self-reflection. Take a moment to think about the beliefs that have been holding you back. Maybe it's the belief that you're not smart enough, talented enough, or deserving of success. Write them down and acknowledge their presence in your life. Remember, it's okay to feel vulnerable during this process. It's all part of the journey toward growth and self-discovery.

Examining the Truth Behind Negative and Restrictive Beliefs:

Here's a secret: most of our negative and restrictive beliefs are not based on facts. They're often distorted perceptions or assumptions we've picked up along the way. So, it's time to challenge their validity. Ask yourself, "Is this belief really true? What evidence supports or disproves it?" Look for alternative perspectives and stories of individuals who have defied similar beliefs. You'll be surprised at how empowering it can be to see that your beliefs are not set in stone.

Shifting Your Mindset:

Now that you're questioning the truth of your beliefs, it's time to shift your mindset. Instead of dwelling on what's holding you back, focus on what's possible. Embrace a growth mindset, where you believe that your abilities and intelligence can be developed through effort and learning. Practice positive self-talk and replace self-limiting thoughts with empowering ones. Remember, you have the power to rewrite your story and create a new narrative that serves your growth and success.

Taking Action to Challenge and Overcome:

It's not enough to just challenge your beliefs in theory; you need to take action. Start small and gradually push yourself outside of your comfort zone. Take on new challenges and prove to yourself that you're capable of more than you think. Celebrate every small victory along the way, as they build your confidence and reinforce the belief that you can overcome any obstacle. Embrace the discomfort, my friend, because that's where real growth happens.

Worksheet: Overcoming Negative and Restrictive Beliefs

1. *Identifying Your Negative and Restrictive Beliefs*

Take a moment to reflect on the beliefs that have been holding you back. Write them down below. Eg I am not smart enough, talented enough, educated enough.

- Belief 1: ________________________________
- Belief 2: _________________________________
- Belief 3: _________________________________
- Belief 4: _________________________________
- Belief 5: _________________________________

Acknowledge the presence of these beliefs in your life and how they have impacted your progress and self-perception.

2. *Examining the Truth Behind Negative and Restrictive Beliefs:*

Challenge the validity of your beliefs by asking yourself the following questions:

- Is this belief really true?
- What evidence supports or disproves it?
- Are there alternative perspectives or stories that defy this belief?

Write down your reflections and any alternative viewpoints you discover:

Belief 1: ________________________________

- Evidence supporting or disproving:

____

- Alternative perspective: ________________________________

Belief 2: ________________________________

- Evidence supporting or disproving:

____

- Alternative perspective: ________________________________

Repeat the process for the remaining beliefs.

3. *Shifting Your Mindset:*

Begin to shift your mindset by focusing on what's possible and adopting a growth mindset. Answer the following:

- What is one empowering thought or affirmation you can use to replace each negative belief?

Belief 1: Empowering thought or affirmation:

____

Belief 2: Empowering thought or affirmation:

____

Belief 3: Empowering thought or affirmation:

____

Belief 4: Empowering thought or affirmation:

____

Belief 5: Empowering thought or affirmation:

____

4. *Taking Action to Challenge and Overcome:*

It's time to take action and challenge your beliefs. Start small and gradually push yourself outside of your comfort zone. Write down specific actions you can take to challenge and overcome your beliefs:

Belief 1: Action steps: ________________________________

Belief 2: Action steps: ________________________________

Belief 3: Action steps: ________________________________

Belief 4: Action steps: ________________________________

Belief 5: Action steps: ________________________________

Celebrate every small victory along the way, and embrace the discomfort as an opportunity for growth.

Remember, this worksheet is designed to guide you on your journey of self-reflection and growth. Take your time, be honest with yourself, and have faith in your ability to overcome these beliefs. You are capable of rewriting your story and creating a life filled with limitless possibilities.

Key Takeaways

1. Negative and restrictive beliefs hold us back from reaching our full potential.

2. Awareness is the first step in challenging these beliefs.

3. Question the validity of your beliefs and seek evidence to disprove them.

4. Cultivate a growth mindset and focus on possibilities and opportunities for growth.

5. Take consistent action and step outside your comfort zone to overcome your limiting beliefs

Action Points to Implement:

1. Identify three negative or restrictive beliefs that are holding you back.

2. Challenge one of these beliefs by seeking evidence that contradicts it.

3. Practice daily positive affirmations to reframe negative thoughts.

4. Set small goals that push you outside your comfort zone and celebrate each achievement.

5. Surround yourself with a supportive community that encourages and uplifts you.

DISCOVER THE POWER OF EMBRACING CHANGE

The Surprising Key to Living Your Best Life

"As the seasons change, so do we. Embracing change is like a tree shedding its leaves, making way for new beginnings and the blossoming of your true self."

Change is an inevitable part of life, and embracing it is crucial for personal growth and development. In this chapter, we will explore the importance of embracing change, understand its various dimensions, and discover how it can help you build your identity, authority, and make fearless decisions.

Overcoming Resistance to Change: Embracing a New Path

Change is an inevitable part of life, yet many people find themselves resisting it. Whether it's in our personal lives or within organizations, the fear and hesitation to embrace change can hold us back from growth and progress. In this section, we will explore the common reasons why even smart homemakers resist change and provide insights on how to overcome these barriers. By understanding these resistances and adopting a mindset of adaptability, we can navigate change more effectively and seize the opportunities it presents.

1. Inertia: Breaking Free from the Familiar

Inertia is like being stuck in our usual routines and not wanting to try something different. To break free from inertia, we need to let go of what's familiar and be open to new possibilities. By doing this, we can grow personally and professionally, and have a more exciting and fulfilling life.

3 ways you can overcome inertia

- Overcoming attachment to the familiar and embracing something new.
- Recognizing that clinging to the past may hinder personal and professional growth.
- Opening ourselves to new possibilities and experiences that enhance our lives.

2. Universalization of the Problem:

Recognize that change doesn't have to start on a large scale—it can begin with small acts. Take these 3 steps so you don’t end up feeling overwhelmed.

- Understanding that change can start with small actions.
- Overcoming resistance by recognizing the potential for positive impact.
- Motivation and determination to initiate change and make a difference.

3. Budget Constraints:

Dealing with limited finances at home can be tough, but there are ways to find creative solutions. By reevaluating how we allocate our resources and exploring innovative approaches, we can make the most of what we have. Whether it's finding cost-effective alternatives or maximizing the use of existing items, thinking creatively helps us overcome budget constraints and create a comfortable and fulfilling home environment.

Let's see

1. Meal planning and cooking at home to save on dining out expenses.

2. Implementing energy-saving habits, such as turning off lights and appliances when not in use, to reduce utility bills.

3. Repurposing and upcycling household items for unique and affordable decor.

4. Utilizing online resources and tutorials for DIY home improvement projects.

5. Creating a budget for groceries and household essentials, and sticking to it.

6. Participating in community swap events or organizing a clothing swap with friends for new wardrobe additions without spending money.

7. Growing a small vegetable or herb garden to save on fresh produce costs.

8. Exploring free or low-cost local activities and events for entertainment.

9. Starting your own enterprise at home and be a support system to your ecosystem.

4. Expanding Perspectives for Misalignment in Vision

Misalignment with vision happens when our initial plans or goals no longer feel right for us. Embracing change means being open to new ideas and possibilities. Let's explore 3 ways you can expand your perspectives

- Questioning common beliefs and broadening our horizons to see things differently. *For example*, focusing on creating a welcoming and comfortable environment rather than obsessing over flawless perfection.

- Reassessing the overarching vision to identify areas for change.

- Exploring new possibilities that align with long-term goals.

5. Home Politics and Fear:

In a home, politics and fear can make it difficult for everyone to openly communicate and collaborate. But by fostering a culture of openness, where everyone feels safe to share their thoughts and feelings without fear of judgment, we create an environment where understanding and collaboration thrive. This leads to better problem-solving and stronger connections among family members. Sharing some doable examples for you to ponder upon

1. Encourage regular family meetngs where everyone has the opportunity to express their thoughts and concerns without fear of judgment.

2. Establish a "no-blame" policy, where mistakes are seen as learning opportunities and open discussion is encouraged to find solutions.

3. Implement active listening techniques, such as summarizing and reflecting, to ensure that everyone's ideas are heard and valued during family discussions.

4. Create a shared family vision or mission statement that encourages collaboration, reminding everyone of the importance of working together towards common goals.

6. Blind Adherence to Home-Based Tradition:

Sometimes, we might follow traditions just because that's how things have always been done. But as homemakers, it's important to evaluate if those practices still work well for our families. By being open to new and innovative ideas, we can find better ways to create a happy and thriving home that meets the changing needs of our loved ones while still preserving what's important to us. *For example,*

- Redesigning living spaces to create multi-functional areas that adapt to evolving needs.

- Embracing modern parenting approaches that focus on empathy and positive discipline.

- Integrating smart home technology for energy efficiency and enhanced convenience.

7. Desire for Genuine Change

Overcoming The desire for genuine change among homemakers arises when they feel previous attempts at change have been superficial or insincere. To overcome resistance, it is important for homemakers to demonstrate the authenticity of proposed changes and highlight how they can make a meaningful difference in their lives and the lives of their families.

For example, as a homemaker, if you've previously attempted to establish a weekly family game night but it felt forced and lacked genuine engagement, you can demonstrate the desire for genuine change by reevaluating the activity. Instead of merely going through the motions, you can have an open conversation with your family, express the importance of quality time, and collaboratively decide on activities that genuinely resonate with everyone's interests and foster meaningful connections. This shift towards authentic engagement can make a significant difference in creating enjoyable and memorable family moments.

To put it mildly, if something is not working and you know it , what's the point of following the same method again and again and crying over it? It's time to find new solutions to the same problems!

Embracing change is a lifelong adventure, and by incorporating the principles and insights shared in this chapter, you can create a meaningful and lasting impact. Approach changes with a friendly and conversational mindset, coupled with a strategic outlook, to open doors to a life brimming with growth, empowerment, and fearlessly making decisions that align with your truest self. Embrace change as your steadfast companion, guiding you along the path towards profound personal fulfillment

Key Takeaways:

1. Change is an inevitable part of life, and embracing it is crucial for personal growth.

2. Overcoming fear and resistance to change requires cultivating a growth mindset and seeking support.

3. Embracing change allows you to build your identity, explore new passions, and assert your authority.

4. Taking ownership of decisions becomes easier when you embrace change and trust your instincts.

5. Navigating major life transitions requires embracing change, self-discovery, and resilience.

Action Points:

1. Cultivate a growth mindset by embracing new experiences and challenging yourself regularly.

2. Seek support from friends, family, or mentors when facing change or making important decisions.

3. Explore new interests and passions to build your identity and authority.

4. Trust your instincts and take ownership of your decisions, even if they involve uncertainty.

5. Embrace change as an opportunity for self-discovery during major life transitions and leverage it for personal growth.

GET WHAT YOU WANT EVERY TIME

The Surprising Secrets of Assertive Negotiation

"Assertiveness is the language of self-respect, spoken with clarity and compassion."

Before we proceed with the chapter, take this small test for yourself!

The Empowered Homemaker's Assert-o-Meter!

Answer the following questions by selecting the most appropriate response (A, B, or C) for each scenario:

1)Your family member asks you to take on an additional household chore that you don't have the capacity for at the moment. Do you:

A) Agree to do it, even if it adds to your workload.

B) Express your inability to take on the task and suggest an alternative solution.

C) Feel frustrated but still agree to do it without voicing your concerns.

2) You have planned a personal activity or outing for yourself, but a friend asks you to cancel your plans and help them with something. Do you:

A) Immediately cancel your plans and prioritize helping your friend.

B) Politely decline and explain that you already have prior commitments.

C) Cancel your plans reluctantly, without expressing your disappointment.

3) During a family discussion, you strongly disagree with an opinion but hesitate to voice your perspective. Do you:

A) Stay quiet and avoid expressing your disagreement.

B) Share your differing opinion respectfully and explain your viewpoint.

C) Give in and agree with the majority opinion, even if you don't fully agree.

4) You lend a valuable item to a neighbour, and they return it damaged. Do you:

A) Accept the item without mentioning the damage, to avoid confrontation.

B) Communicate your disappointment about the damage and request a resolution.

C) Ignore the damage and pretend it doesn't bother you.

5) A family member consistently interrupts or talks over you during conversations. Do you:

A) Remain silent and let them dominate the conversation.

B) Assertively ask for your turn to speak and express your thoughts.

C) Continue talking without addressing the interruptions.

I hope you did this exercise, it's simple yet powerful.

Score Interpretation:

5-7 points: Low assertiveness - You tend to avoid conflict and prioritize others' needs over your own.

8-12 points: Moderate assertiveness - You sometimes express your opinions and set boundaries but may struggle at times.

13-15 points: High assertiveness - You confidently communicate your needs, set boundaries, and express yourself effectively.

Understanding Assertiveness:

Assertiveness is the art of expressing oneself confidently and respectfully while respecting the rights and boundaries of others. By practicing assertiveness, you can enhance your self-esteem, improve communication, and foster healthier relationships. It's important to differentiate assertiveness from aggression and passivity, as assertiveness lies in the middle ground, empowering you to voice your thoughts and needs without steamrolling others.

Communication is key, and assertiveness plays a crucial role in expressing ourselves politely yet firmly. In this chapter, we'll explore tools and techniques that will help you live harmoniously, respecting yourself without hurting others. It's important to avoid being rude under the guise of frankness or disregarding others' words, which only leads to anger. Instead, let's foster a culture of mutual respect, where we uplift one another

Recognizing and Overcoming Barriers to Assertiveness:

Two types of barriers can hinder our ability to be assertive. Internal barriers, such as low self-esteem, fear of conflict, or the tendency to please others, need to be acknowledged and addressed. External barriers, like cultural norms and societal expectations, may also influence our assertiveness. By identifying and overcoming these barriers, you can cultivate a stronger sense of assertiveness.

Developing Assertive Communication Skills:

Assertive communication is the foundation of practicing assertiveness. Active listening and empathy are key skills that demonstrate respect and understanding. Effective techniques, such as "I" statements and assertive body language, can help you express your thoughts, feelings, and boundaries confidently and clearly. Let's learn how to do that, shall we?

Example 1: Dealing with family members scattering things around and you cleaning up after them.

Imagine a scenario where a family member consistently leaves their belongings scattered around the house, causing inconvenience to others. Here's how you can assertively address the situation:

1. Use "I" statements: Express your feelings and needs using statements like, "I feel frustrated when there are items left out because it makes it difficult for everyone to move around."

2. Provide a specific request: Make a clear and reasonable request, such as, "Could you please make an effort to put your belongings in their designated places to ensure a tidy living space?"

3. Validate their perspective: Acknowledge their point of view by saying, "I understand you may be busy or forgetful, but it would greatly help if we all contribute to maintaining a clean environment."

4. Suggest a solution: Collaboratively find a solution that works for everyone, like implementing a designated area for personal belongings or setting a reminder to tidy up regularly.

Example 2: Dealing with Difficult Family Members Using Assertive Communication

In a scenario where a family member constantly criticizes and puts you down, you can respond assertively using these simple steps:

1. Stay calm and composed: Take a deep breath and maintain your composure before addressing the situation.

2. Express your feelings: Use "I" statements to communicate how their behaviour affects you. For example, say, "I feel hurt and demotivated when you constantly criticize my efforts."

3. Set boundaries: Clearly state your limits by saying, "I would appreciate it if you could refrain from making negative comments about my actions or decisions."

4. Request respect: Politely ask for respectful communication, such as, "I kindly request that we maintain a supportive and constructive environment within our family."

5. Focus on positive solutions: Shift the conversation towards finding constructive solutions or alternatives.

Example 3: Your family member frequently interrupts you while you're speaking, disregarding your thoughts and opinions.

Your Assertive Response:

1. Stay composed: Maintain your calm and avoid reacting impulsively to the interruptions.

2. Address the behaviour: Assertively point out the issue by saying, "I've noticed that I often get interrupted while expressing my thoughts."

3. Express your feelings: Share how it makes you feel using "I" statements, such as, "I feel unheard and disrespected when I'm constantly interrupted."

4. Request active listening: Politely ask for their attention and uninterrupted time to speak, saying, "I would appreciate it if you could let me finish my thoughts before responding."

5. Seek collaboration: Emphasize the importance of open and respectful communication, suggesting, "Let's work together to create an environment where we can all express ourselves fully and listen attentively to one another."

Example 5: Resolving a Disagreement with a Colleague in a professional setting. You and a colleague have differing opinions on how to approach a project.

1. Active Listening: Begin by actively listening to your colleague's perspective without interrupting. Show that you respect their opinion and value their input.

2. "I" Statements: Express your own thoughts and concerns using "I" statements. For example, say, "I believe that our approach should focus more on X aspect because of Y reasons."

3. Find Common Ground: Look for areas of agreement or shared goals. Emphasize that both of you want the project to succeed and find ways to align your approaches.

4. Collaborative Problem-Solving: Explore potential compromises or alternative solutions that incorporate both perspectives. Brainstorm together and consider the pros and cons of each suggestion.

5. Reach Consensus: Aim for a mutually agreeable solution. It may require some negotiation and willingness to find a middle ground that satisfies both parties.

Key points to keep in mind while practicing assertive communication

Express your feelings and needs directly: Clearly state your thoughts, emotions, and requirements without beating around the bush. Avoid excessive language or ambiguity.

Use "I" statements: Take ownership of your emotions and opinions by using "I" statements. For example, say, "I feel disappointed" instead of "You always let me down."

Stick to the facts: Focus on presenting the facts of a situation rather than making assumptions or speculating about others' intentions. This helps to keep the conversation grounded and avoids unnecessary conflicts.

Maintain respectful body language: Pay attention to your body language, as it plays a significant role in how your message is received. Stand tall, maintain eye contact, and keep an open and relaxed posture to show respect for both yourself and the other person.

Practice active listening: Actively listen to others by giving them your undivided attention, maintaining eye contact, and genuinely seeking to understand their perspective. Respond thoughtfully and avoid interrupting or dismissing their thoughts.

Validate others' perspectives: Even if you disagree with someone, acknowledge and validate their perspective. Show empathy and understanding, as this can foster open and constructive communication. You are free to disagree respectfully!

Practice self-care and self-compassion: Assertive communication starts with self-respect and self-care. Prioritize your well-being and practice self-compassion. Recognize that it's okay to assert your needs and feelings while also considering the needs of others.

ARCH Technique of Assertiveness

I totally understand that remembering how to communicate assertively can seem challenging at first. But don't worry, I've got just the technique to make it easier for you – it's called the ARCH Technique!

Imagine this: You're having a conversation, and you want to express yourself confidently and respectfully. Well, just think of ARCH like a sturdy bridge that helps you navigate through that conversation smoothly.

A - Assertive Expression:

- Clearly state your thoughts, feelings, and needs.
- Use "I" statements to take ownership of your perspective.
- Avoid excessive language and ambiguity.

R - Respectful Body Language:

- Maintain a relaxed but confident posture.
- Keep eye contact and actively listen to the other person.
- Use open gestures and uncrossed arms to show receptiveness.

C - Consistent Boundaries:

- Define and communicate your personal boundaries clearly.

- Be consistent in upholding and enforcing your boundaries.
- Respect others' boundaries as well.

H - Healthy Problem-Solving:

- Approach conflicts with a problem-solving mindset.
- Collaborate and find mutually beneficial solutions.
- Focus on resolving the issue rather than placing blame.

With the ARCH Technique, you'll be equipped to communicate assertively with confidence and respect. So, go ahead, give it a try, and watch your communication skills soar!

Key Takeaways:

Assertiveness is expressing oneself confidently and respectfully while respecting others.

Overcome internal and external barriers to cultivate assertiveness.

Develop assertive communication skills, including active listening and using "I" statements.

Apply assertiveness in personal relationships, workplace dynamics, and decision-making.

Nurturing self-confidence and self-worth is essential for practicing assertiveness.

Action Points:

Practice assertive communication by expressing your thoughts and needs openly and respectfully.

Set clear boundaries in your relationships and communicate them assertively.

Take small steps to assert yourself in professional settings, such as offering your opinions or negotiating for what you deserve.

Embrace assertive decision-making by trusting your intuition and making choices confidently.

Cultivate self-confidence and self-worth through positive affirmations, self-care, and celebrating your assertiveness successes.

MASTERING THE ART OF CONTINUOUS GROWTH

Empowering Yourself through Personal and Professional Growth

"Embrace the dance of self-improvement, for with each step forward, we sculpt our own destiny and become architects of our dreams."

Let's explore the importance of continuous growth, identify avenues for personal and professional development, and provide strategies for embracing these opportunities.

The Value of Personal and Professional Development:

Personal and professional development is the key to unlocking your full potential and living a fulfilling life. By continuously seeking growth, you enhance your skills, expand your knowledge, and cultivate a growth mindset. Personal and professional development are intertwined, as they complement each other and lead to holistic growth and success.

Assessing Personal and Professional Needs:

Before embarking on a development journey, it is crucial to assess your personal and professional needs. Reflect on your strengths, weaknesses, and areas for improvement. Identify your professional goals and aspirations, aligning them with your personal growth objectives. By understanding your needs, you can set clear priorities and tailor your development efforts accordingly.

Assessing personal and professional needs is a crucial step in the journey of personal and professional development. It helps individuals identify areas for improvement and set clear priorities. Here are a few examples of how one can assess their personal and professional needs:

Self-Reflection and Feedback:

Take time to reflect on your strengths, weaknesses, and areas where you feel you need improvement. Consider what skills or knowledge gaps may be holding you back from reaching your goals. Additionally, seek feedback from trusted friends, mentors, or colleagues who can provide an outside perspective on your personal and professional attributes.

Example: You might realize through self-reflection and feedback that you have excellent communication skills but lack proficiency in project management. This assessment highlights the need to focus on improving your project management abilities.

SWOT Analysis:

Conduct a SWOT (Strengths, Weaknesses, Opportunities, Threats) analysis to assess your personal and professional landscape. Identify your strengths, such as specific skills or traits that set you apart, as well as your weaknesses or areas where you face challenges. Explore potential opportunities that align with your goals, and consider the external threats or obstacles that may hinder your progress.

Example: In a SWOT analysis, you might discover that your organizational skills are a strength, but you struggle with public speaking (a weakness). This analysis helps you recognize the need to address public speaking skills to seize future opportunities and overcome potential threats.

Exploring Personal Development Opportunities:

Personal development is a lifelong journey of self-discovery and self-improvement. Seek opportunities for self-reflection and self-awareness through journaling, meditation, or therapy. Surround yourself with mentors and role models who inspire you. Engage in personal growth activities such as reading books, attending workshops, or exploring new hobbies. Embrace these opportunities to expand your horizons and nurture your personal growth.

Navigating Professional Development Opportunities:

Professional development is essential for advancing your career and staying relevant in a rapidly changing world. Identify areas for professional growth and skill enhancement. Explore educational opportunities such as courses, certifications, or even pursuing higher degrees. Network with professionals in your field and actively seek challenging projects and new responsibilities. By embracing these opportunities, you can sharpen your skills and broaden your professional horizons.

Overcoming Obstacles and Challenges:

The journey of personal and professional development may come with its share of obstacles and challenges. Time constraints, fear of failure, and external barriers such as financial limitations may pose challenges. However, by managing your time effectively, embracing a growth mindset, and seeking support from mentors and peers, you can overcome these obstacles. Develop resilience, persistence, and a strategic mindset to navigate the challenges along your development path.

Creating a Personalized Development Plan:

A personalized development plan acts as a roadmap to guide your growth journey. Set SMART (Specific, Measurable, Achievable, Relevant, Time-bound) goals that align with your aspirations. Break down these goals into actionable steps, creating a clear path for progress. Regularly assess your progress, make adjustments, and celebrate milestones along the way. By having a well-defined plan, you can stay focused and motivated throughout your development journey.

Integrating Development into Daily Life:

Make learning a habit by dedicating time each day to acquire new knowledge and skills. Create an environment that supports your growth, such as joining communities of like-minded individuals or participating in mastermind groups. Seek feedback from mentors, peers, or colleagues, as it fosters continuous improvement. Lastly, prioritize self-care and nurture your well-being during the development process, as self-care is vital for sustainable growth.

Balancing Personal and Professional Development:

Finding a balance between personal and professional development is crucial for holistic growth. Establish boundaries and manage your priorities effectively. Seek alignment between your personal and professional goals to ensure they support and complement each other. Recognize that personal and professional development are interconnected, and growth in one area can positively impact the other.

Key Takeaways:

1. Personal and professional development are essential for unlocking your potential and leading a fulfilling life.

2. Assess your needs and set clear priorities for personal and professional growth.

3. Embrace personal development opportunities through self-reflection, mentorship, and exploration of new activities.

4. Navigate professional development by seeking educational opportunities, networking, and embracing challenges.

5. Create a personalized development plan, integrate growth into daily life, and find a balance between personal and professional aspirations.

Action Points:

1. Spend 10 minutes each day on personal development activities such as reading, journaling, or meditation.

2. Seek out a mentor or role model who can guide and inspire you in your personal and professional growth.

3. Enrol in a course or certification program to enhance your professional skills and knowledge.

4. Set one challenging goal related to personal or professional development and create a step-by-step plan to achieve it.

5. Prioritize self-care by dedicating time for relaxation, exercise, and nurturing your well-being.

CONNECT-INSPIRE- SUCCEED

How to Find Growth-Minded Connections

"Networking is the art of cultivating meaningful connections, where each encounter becomes a stepping stone on the path to personal and collective growth."

In this chapter, we will explore the power of building a supportive network, engaging in community, and connecting with growth-minded individuals.

A supportive network is a group of individuals who uplift and encourage us on our personal growth journey. They provide emotional support, guidance, and constructive feedback. When combined with growth-minded connections, these relationships become an unstoppable force that fuels our aspirations and propels us towards success. Recognizing the impact of such a network is crucial for realizing our potential and achieving our goals.

Identifying Your Supportive Network and Growth-Minded Connections:

Begin by assessing your current relationships and connections. Identify individuals who align with your values and aspirations, genuinely support your growth, and possess growth-minded qualities. Nurturing existing relationships and forging new ones is essential. Seek out like-minded individuals who inspire and challenge you, and who believe in your abilities.

Building Trust, Reciprocity, and Authority:

Trust is the cornerstone of any supportive network and growth-minded connections. Cultivate trust by being authentic, reliable, and respectful in your interactions. Remember that relationships are a two-way street. Practice reciprocity by offering support and assistance to others in your network. Establish your authority in your chosen field by showcasing your expertise, sharing knowledge, and engaging in industry-related discussions.

Engaging in Community Activities

Participating in community activities provides numerous benefits for personal growth. Look for communities and groups aligned with your interests and goals, particularly growth-minded communities. Actively engage in events, workshops, and volunteer opportunities, both online and offline. By immersing yourself in these communities, you broaden your horizons, gain new perspectives, and develop valuable connections.

Networking Strategies

Leverage the power of online platforms and social media to expand your network. Join professional groups, forums, and communities where you can connect with like-minded individuals. Attend conferences, workshops, and industry events to meet and learn from experts in your field. Consider joining professional organizations and associations that offer networking opportunities tailored to educated, growth-seeking homemakers.

Leveraging Mentorship and Coaching:

Mentors and coaches play a crucial role in personal development. Seek out mentors and coaches within your network or community who can guide and support you on your journey. Establish effective mentorship and coaching relationships by being open to feedback, setting clear goals, and maintaining regular communication. Embrace the wisdom and guidance that mentors offer, as they can significantly accelerate your growth.

Overcoming Challenges, Embracing Vulnerability, and Building Resilience:

Setbacks and obstacles are inevitable in our personal growth journey. During challenging times, rely on your support system and growth-minded connections for encouragement and advice. Embrace vulnerability by sharing your struggles openly, as it fosters deeper connections. By facing challenges together, you build resilience and develop the strength to overcome any hurdles that come your way.

Celebrating Successes, making a Difference, and Giving Back:

Don't forget to celebrate your successes along the way. Acknowledge and appreciate your achievements, no matter how big or small. Share your successes with your supportive network, growth-minded connections, and community, inspiring others with your progress. Additionally, contribute to the growth and well-being of others. Offer your support, knowledge, and skills to uplift those around you, making a positive impact in your community and beyond.

Connecting with Growth-Minded Individuals:

Connecting with growth-minded individuals is an incredible opportunity for personal growth and empowerment. These individuals possess traits that contribute to their development, such as embracing challenges, seeking learning opportunities, and maintaining a positive outlook. To connect with them, establish your identity and authority in your field, find growth-minded communities, leverage networking strategies, engage in meaningful conversations, and embrace vulnerability and authenticity.

Key Takeaways:

1. Building a supportive network and connecting with growth-minded individuals are essential for personal growth and empowerment.

2. Actively engage in community activities and seek out growth-minded communities aligned with your interests and goals.

3. Establish trust, reciprocity, and authority within your network and connections.

4. Leverage networking strategies, both online and offline, to expand your connections.

5. Seek mentorship and coaching from growth-minded individuals to accelerate your personal development.

Action Points:

1. Assess your current relationships and identify individuals who support your growth and possess growth-minded qualities.

2. Participate in at least one community activity or event each month, focusing on growth-minded communities.

3. Reach out to someone in your network or growth-minded connections and offer support or assistance.

4. Join online professional groups or forums, engaging in meaningful discussions.

5. Seek out a mentor or coach who aligns with your growth mindset and can guide you in your personal growth journey.

THE MIND-BLOWING MIRROR THAT MANIFESTS YOUR WILDEST DREAMS

Unleashing Your Inner Power and Abundance

"The power to shape your destiny lies within the choices you make and the actions you take."

In a quaint village nestled at the foot of a majestic mountain, there lived a young woman named Isabella. She possessed a heart full of dreams and an unwavering determination to create a life that resonated with purpose and fulfillment. However, like many others, she often found herself hesitant and unsure of how to embark on the journey that lay before her.

One cloudy afternoon, as Isabella explored the attic of her ancestral home, she stumbled upon an old, ornate mirror concealed beneath a dusty, moth-eaten sheet. The mirror, adorned with intricate carvings and shimmering with an otherworldly glow, seemed to beckon her closer. Curiosity consumed her, and she reached out to remove the sheet, revealing the mirror's captivating beauty.

As Isabella stared into the reflective surface, she marvelled at her own appearance and imagined how beautiful her life could be. Just as the thought formed in her mind, a knock came upon her door. Opening it, Isabella was surprised to find a young man standing there, presenting her with beautiful clothes and jewels. He professed his love for her and asked for her hand in marriage. Overjoyed, Isabella danced in joy and accepted his proposal, feeling like her dreams were coming true.

Holding the mirror once again, she admired her smiling reflection but suddenly had a nagging thought. What if something bad happened, and her happiness vanished? In that moment, she heard a scream from downstairs. Rushing to investigate, Isabella discovered that her mother had fallen and fractured her leg. Fear gripped her, and she wondered if the mirror had somehow caused this misfortune.

Isabella looked into the mirror again, hoping for reassurance. As she saw her image, she thought of how amazing her life was and how everything had worked out for her. Just then, her brother entered the door and delivered the news that their mother was fine, and it was just a minor injury. Isabella became convinced that the mirror possessed some sort of magic and that she had stumbled upon something magnificent.

Every day thereafter, Isabella made a conscious effort to get ready, smile, and ask for what she truly wanted. She discovered that when she asked with unwavering belief, things began to manifest. Recognizing this pattern, she wrote down a list of her desires and followed this practice every single day.

One day, Isabella's grandmother confronted her about her peculiar behaviour. Isabella hesitantly shared everything, hoping her grandmother would understand. To her surprise, her grandmother led her to an even bigger mirror, a grand and magnificent model of the smaller one. Isabella squealed with delight, realizing she could ask for anything and it would come to her.

She decided to try it immediately and, as if by magic, footsteps could be heard approaching her door. It was the King himself, arriving right at her doorstep, and the entire household rejoiced in greeting their beloved ruler. Tears of joy filled their eyes as they celebrated the glorious occasion throughout the day.

The next day, Isabella approached her grandmother, yearning to use the mirror once again. But her grandmother had sombre news. The mirror had been broken, shattered beyond repair. Isabella went into a state of shock, unable to eat or sleep for an entire week. Her dreams seemed shattered along with the mirror, and despair consumed her.

Finally, after ten days, Isabella mustered the strength to rise again, though still plagued by despair. Desperately hoping to reclaim the magic mirror, she sought solace from her grandmother. Once more, her grandmother had surprising words for her—words that shook Isabella's world to its core.

Her grandmother explained that the mirror was ordinary and that the extraordinary power resided within Isabella herself. It was her thoughts, her beliefs, and her actions that were truly creating the life she desired. All she needed to do was choose what she wanted, believe in herself, and take action.

Isabella initially looked at her grandmother with anger, feeling deceived. However, her grandmother's loving gaze softened her heart, and she decided to give it another try. Though confused and uncertain, Isabella followed her grandmother's guidance, dressing up, smiling, and energetically asking for what she desired. She wrote it down and started with small things.

Isabella, a sweet and determined soul, didn't want to hurt her grandmother, so she persisted, even in her doubt. And gradually, the magic began to return. One wish after another started coming true, and Isabella's confidence in herself grew stronger. She realized that the true magic resided within her all along.

From that day forward, Isabella made a conscious effort to create an extraordinary and fulfilling life. She embraced her innate power and used it to its maximum potential. After all, life is lived only once, and Isabella was determined to make the most of her gift.

The Power of Self-Investment:

Investing in yourself is a recognition of your inherent worth and value. It involves prioritizing self-care, embracing lifelong learning, and cultivating self-confidence. By investing in yourself, you lay the foundation for personal growth and create a strong sense of self.

Building Your Identity and Authority:

Investing in yourself starts with building your identity and authority. Cultivate self-confidence and self-belief, and define your values, passions, and goals. Establishing your personal brand and expertise allows you to stand out and make a meaningful impact in your chosen field.

Investing in Education and Skill Development:

Continual education and skill development are crucial aspects of self-investment. Pursue formal education or certifications, seek opportunities for skill enhancement, and embrace continuous learning through books, courses, and workshops. By investing in your knowledge and skills, you equip yourself with the tools necessary to thrive in your personal and professional life.

Prioritizing Mental and Emotional Well-being:

Your mental and emotional well-being are integral to your overall self-investment. Practice self-care and stress management techniques, seek therapy or counselling when needed, and nurture healthy relationships and boundaries. Prioritizing your mental and emotional health enables you to navigate life's challenges with resilience and clarity.

Financial Investment in Yourself:

Managing your finances wisely is an essential aspect of self-investment. Create a budget, save for personal and professional growth, and invest in financial education and literacy. Explore investment options that align with your goals to build long-term wealth and financial security.

Investing in Physical Health and Fitness:

Physical health is a valuable asset that deserves your attention. Prioritize regular exercise and a balanced diet, seek preventive healthcare and regular check-ups, and incorporate healthy habits into your lifestyle. By investing in your physical health, you enhance your energy, vitality, and overall well-being.

Time Management and Productivity:

Effective time management and productivity strategies enable you to make the most of your days. Set goals, prioritize tasks, and develop time management skills. Embrace productivity tools and techniques that help you stay focused and organized, allowing you to maximize your productivity and achieve your desired outcomes.

Building a Supportive Network:

Surrounding yourself with positive and growth-minded individuals is a key aspect of self-investment. Seek mentorship and guidance from role models, engage in communities and networking events, and nurture relationships that uplift and inspire you. A supportive network provides invaluable support, guidance, and opportunities for personal growth.

Taking Risks and Embracing Growth Opportunities:

Investing in yourself often requires taking risks and embracing growth opportunities. Step out of your comfort zone, embrace challenges as opportunities for learning and development, and overcome fear by taking calculated risks. By pushing your boundaries, you unlock new possibilities and accelerate your personal growth journey

Key Takeaways:

1. Recognize your inherent worth and value, and prioritize yourself.
2. Continuously invest in education, skills, and personal development.
3. Prioritize your mental and emotional well-being for resilience and clarity.
4. Manage your finances wisely and invest in your financial literacy.
5. Take care of your physical health, practice effective time management, build a supportive network, and embrace growth opportunities.

Action Points:

1. Identify one area of personal growth you want to invest in and set specific goals.

2. Allocate time and resources for learning and skill development regularly.

3. Incorporate self-care practices into your daily routine and seek support when needed.

4. Create a financial plan that includes saving and investing for your future.

5. Step out of your comfort zone by taking on a new challenge or pursuing a growth opportunity.

GUIDING LIGHTS

The Power of Mentorship

"Mentorship is the art of unlocking doors that were once invisible, allowing you to step into a world of growth, enlightenment, and endless possibilities."

While embarking on a journey of growth and success, seek mentorship from seasoned individuals, it's a game-changer. Their guidance and wisdom unlock a wealth of insights, helping you overcome obstacles and accelerate your progress just like Isabella's grandmother become her mentor who helped her unleash her true potential.

The Benefits of Mentorship:

Mentorship offers a multitude of benefits. By connecting with experienced individuals, you gain access to their wisdom, expertise, and networks. Mentors provide guidance, support, and valuable feedback, helping you navigate obstacles and make informed decisions. Embracing mentorship can significantly enhance your personal and professional growth.

Identifying Your Mentorship Needs:

To find the right mentor, it's important to identify your specific needs. Assess your goals, challenges, and areas for growth. Consider the skills, knowledge, and qualities you seek in a mentor-mentee relationship. By understanding your needs, you can better align with a mentor who can provide the guidance you require.

Finding the Right Mentor:

Finding a mentor may involve tapping into your existing network, reaching out to professional associations, or exploring online platforms and mentorship programs. Look for individuals who align with your values, possess the expertise you desire, and demonstrate a willingness to support your growth. Remember, the right mentor can have a profound impact on your journey.

The mistake I often see people make is hesitating to ask, and even if they do, they sometimes approach the wrong person. How can someone who has not walked the path show you the way? It's important to overcome this hesitation and seek out mentors who have relevant experience and can provide valuable guidance based on their own journey.

Building a Successful Mentor-Mentee Relationship:

Once you've found a potential mentor, approach them with respect and genuine interest. Clearly communicate your expectations and goals for the mentorship. Nurture the relationship by actively participating in discussions, seeking feedback, and showing gratitude for their guidance. A strong mentor-mentee relationship is built on trust, mutual respect, and open communication.

Leveraging Mentorship for Personal Growth:

Take advantage of your mentor's experiences and insights. Seek guidance in decision-making processes, learn from their successes and failures, and apply their wisdom to your own journey. Embrace constructive feedback as an opportunity for growth. Remember, your mentor is there to support and empower you.

Active Engagement and Learning from Mentors:

Make the most of your mentorship by actively engaging in sessions and discussions. Prepare thoughtful questions, seek clarification, and take ownership of your learning. Remember, mentorship is a two-way street—your active participation enhances the value of the experience.

Overcoming Challenges in Mentorship:

Mentorship may come with challenges such as time constraints or misalignments in expectations. Manage your time effectively, be respectful of your mentor's availability, and find a schedule that works for both of you. Address any conflicts or concerns openly and honestly, and be willing to adapt the mentorship approach if needed.

Giving Back and Paying It Forward:

Express gratitude to your mentors for their guidance and support. Show appreciation for their investment in your growth. As you progress in your journey, share your knowledge and experiences with others. Become a mentor yourself and contribute to a culture of mentorship. By paying it forward, you create a ripple effect of growth and empowerment.

Key Takeaways:

1. Seek mentorship to gain valuable insights and support for your personal and professional growth.

2. Identify your specific mentorship needs and align with mentors who can provide guidance in those areas.

3. Build a strong mentor-mentee relationship based on trust, respect, and open communication.

4. Leverage your mentor's experiences and feedback to accelerate your learning and decision-making processes.

5. Give back by expressing gratitude to your mentors and becoming a mentor yourself, creating a cycle of growth and empowerment.

Action Points:

1. Reflect on your goals and challenges, and identify one area where mentorship could make a significant impact.

2. Reach out to potential mentors within your network or professional associations,

expressing your interest in their guidance.

3. Clearly communicate your expectations and goals for the mentorship relationship.

4. Actively engage in mentorship sessions, seeking feedback and applying insights to your own journey.

5. When the time is right, consider becoming a mentor to others, sharing your knowledge and experiences for their growth.

MASTER YOUR MONEY MINDSET

Letting Go of Guilt to Manifest True Prosperity

"Our beliefs about money are the walls we construct around our potential, and by questioning them, we open the doors to a world of financial liberation."

Understanding Money Guilt

Money guilt refers to the feeling of shame, regret, or unease associated with money and financial matters. It arises when individuals experience negative emotions or beliefs related to their financial situation, spending habits, or financial success. Money guilt can manifest in various ways and impact different aspects of a person's life.

Causes of Money Guilt:

1. Upbringing and Beliefs: Our upbringing and early experiences with money can shape our beliefs and attitudes towards it. If we were raised in an environment that emphasized scarcity or taught us that money is inherently bad, we may develop guilt when we have more than others or when we spend on ourselves.

Example: Someone who grew up in a family struggling with financial difficulties might feel guilty about pursuing wealth or spending money on personal desires because they associate it with selfishness or extravagance.

2. Comparison and Social Pressure: Comparing ourselves to others and societal expectations can contribute to money guilt. Seeing others in need or struggling financially can lead to guilt when we have more resources or financial stability.

Example: A person might feel guilty for spending money on luxuries like vacations or designer items because they compare themselves to friends or family members who are struggling financially.

3. Fear of Judgement: Fear of being judged by others for our financial choices can also create money guilt. Concerns about what others think of our spending habits or financial success can cause guilt and inhibit us from making choices aligned with our values and desires.

Example: Someone might feel guilty about pursuing a high-paying job or career advancement because they fear being seen as materialistic or greedy by their peers.

4. Past Financial Mistakes: Regret from past financial decisions or mistakes can contribute to money guilt. If we have made poor choices or experienced financial loss in the past, we may feel guilty about our ability to handle money effectively.

Example: A person who made a significant investment that resulted in a loss may feel guilty about their decision-making skills and doubt their ability to manage money responsibly.

5. Societal Messages: Cultural or societal messages that equate money with negative traits, such as greed or corruption, can lead to money guilt. These messages can create conflicting emotions about financial success and hinder personal growth.

Example: Someone who has achieved financial success through their business may feel guilty about their wealth because they believe that it goes against the idea of leading a virtuous or humble life.

Challenging Beliefs and Mindsets:

We often adopt societal beliefs about money without questioning them. By challenging these beliefs and examining our own self-limiting beliefs, we can break free from their grip. It's time to cultivate a growth mindset when it comes to money and see it as a tool for personal growth rather than a source of guilt.

Shifting Perspectives on Wealth:

Wealth goes beyond material possessions. It includes financial security, abundance, and the freedom to pursue our passions. By redefining wealth and recognizing its positive impact on our lives, we can release the guilt associated with desiring and achieving financial success.

Releasing Shame and Judgment:

Shame and judgment only weigh us down and prevent us from making progress. We must acknowledge and release any shame we feel about our financial situation or decisions. Let go of judgment towards ourselves and others, and instead, cultivate self-compassion and acceptance regarding our relationship with money.

Building Financial Literacy and Empowerment:

One way to overcome money guilt is by gaining knowledge and understanding about personal finance. Educate yourself, seek resources, and develop financial literacy. Empowerment comes from taking control of your finances and making informed decisions.

Shifting Focus to Purpose and Values:

Money guilt often arises when we lose sight of our values and purpose. Reflect on your personal values and ensure that your financial decisions align with them. Shift your focus from material possessions to the fulfillment and joy that come from spending and saving with purpose.

Practicing Gratitude and Abundance:

Gratitude is a powerful antidote to money guilt. Embrace a mindset of gratitude for the financial resources you have, no matter how big or small. Cultivate an abundance mentality and believe in your ability to attract and create more wealth. Regularly engage in gratitude practices to release money guilt and invite prosperity into your life. We will look at this in more detail in the chapter on Gratitude

Making Conscious Financial Decisions:

To overcome money guilt, it's crucial to make conscious financial decisions. Develop a decision-making framework that considers your goals, values, and long-term aspirations. Take ownership of your financial choices and embrace the outcomes, learning and growing from any mistakes along the way.

Key Takeaways:

1. Recognize and acknowledge the presence of money guilt in your life.

2. Challenge societal and self-limiting beliefs about money.

3. Redefine wealth beyond material possessions and embrace its positive impact.

4. Cultivate self-compassion and release shame and judgment towards yourself and others.

5. Take proactive steps to build financial literacy, make conscious financial decisions, and embrace a growth mindset with money.

Action Points

Question and challenge your beliefs about money.

Expand your definition of wealth beyond material possessions.

Treat yourself with kindness and understanding regarding your financial situation.

Take proactive steps to educate yourself about personal finance.

Ensure your financial choices align with your values and priorities.

THE PROFITABLE PURSUIT

Monetizing Your Skills for Sustainable Success

"Monetizing your skills is not just about financial gain, but also about unlocking the full potential of your unique talents and making a meaningful impact in the world."

In this chapter, we will explore how to discover your skills and passions, assess market demand, develop expertise, choose a monetization strategy, and build a strong brand presence. Let's dive in and unlock the potential of turning your passions into profit.

Discovering Your Skills and Passions:

Take some time to reflect on your strengths, talents, and skills. What activities bring you joy and a sense of fulfillment? Identify the intersection between your skills and passions to uncover monetization opportunities that align with your true self.

Assessing Market Demand and Viability:

Research is key to understanding market trends and potential opportunities. Evaluate the demand and profitability of your skills and passions. Consider factors such as competition, target audience, and scalability to determine the viability of your monetization venture.

Developing Your Expertise:

Continuously improve and refine your skills. Seek additional education or training if needed. Build a portfolio or track record that demonstrates your expertise in your chosen area. The more you invest in developing your skills, the more valuable and marketable they become.

Don't make the mistake of abandoning everything just because you got married or had children. That is not a reason to cease pursuing your passions and honing your abilities. You can still provide support to your ecosystem, work from home, and earn money that adds to your bank account. Choose your profession wisely and make sure it aligns with your aspirations.

In addition to developing your talent-supporting skills, it is crucial to acquire business skills to effectively grow your business. Nowadays, digital skills and business skills are essential competencies one must possess.

As homemakers, we need to continually upgrade our skills and understand how the market operates and the language it speaks. I will touch on some topics to help you gain a better understanding.

Creating a Value Proposition:

Clearly define the unique value you offer to clients or customers. Identify your target audience and understand their needs. Craft a compelling message that communicates the benefits of your skills and passions. Your value proposition will set you apart from the competition and attract the right customers.

Choosing a Monetization Strategy:

Explore different monetization models such as offering services, creating products, or implementing subscription-based models. Select the strategy that best suits your skills, passions, and target market. Consider pricing, distribution channels, and marketing tactics to maximize your monetization efforts.

Building Your Brand and Online Presence:

Establish a strong personal brand that reflects your skills and passions. Create a professional website or online platform to showcase your offerings. Leverage social media and digital marketing to reach your target audience. Consistency and authenticity in your brand will attract loyal customers and increase your visibility.

Networking and Collaborations:

Build relationships with industry professionals and potential clients. Seek collaborations and partnerships to expand your reach. Participate in relevant communities and events to enhance your visibility and open doors to new opportunities. Networking is a powerful tool for growth and expanding your monetization prospects. An entire chapter has been dedicated to this subject as you will need support to propel forward.

Marketing and Promotion:

Develop a comprehensive marketing strategy to attract clients or customers. Utilize online and offline marketing channels effectively. Leverage content marketing, social media, and advertising to promote your skills and passions. Consistent and targeted marketing efforts will help you reach a wider audience and generate leads.

Building Client Relationships and Providing Value:

Nurture client relationships through effective communication and exceptional service. Go above and beyond to exceed customer expectations. Continuously adapt and improve based on client feedback and market trends. Building strong relationships and delivering value will lead to customer loyalty and referrals.

Managing Finances and Scaling Your Business:

Establish a solid financial plan and track your income and expenses. Invest in resources and tools to streamline operations and increase productivity. Explore opportunities for scaling your business, such as expanding your offerings or entering new markets. Smart financial management and strategic scaling are essential for long-term success.

Overcoming Challenges and Staying Motivated:

Acknowledge that challenges are part of the journey. Address common obstacles and setbacks with resilience and a growth mindset. Cultivate self-motivation by setting goals, celebrating milestones, and surrounding yourself with a supportive network. Stay focused on your passion and purpose, and remember that every challenge is an opportunity for growth.

Monetizing your skills and passions is a transformative endeavour that can lead to both personal fulfillment and financial independence. By discovering your unique abilities, understanding market demand, developing expertise, and building a strong brand presence, you can turn your passions into a profitable venture. Take action, believe in yourself, and unlock the potential within you.

Key Takeaways:

1. Reflect on your skills and passions to discover monetization opportunities that align with your true self.

2. Research market demand and viability to assess the profitability of your skills and passions.

3. Continuously develop your expertise to increase your value and marketability.

4. Craft a compelling value proposition that communicates the benefits of your skills to your target audience.

5. Build a strong brand presence, network, and market your skills and passions effectively to attract customers and clients.

Action Points

Conduct a Skills and Passions Inventory: Identify your top three skills or passions with monetization potential.

Research and Identify a Niche Market: Deep dive into your skills or passions to find specific target audiences or customer segments.

Set Clear and Achievable Goals: Define specific goals and break them down into actionable steps.

Create a Personal Brand Strategy: Develop a strategy to establish a strong personal brand, including unique selling points and a compelling brand story.

Start Networking and Building Connections: Engage with professionals and potential clients, attending events, joining communities, and seeking collaborations or mentorship opportunities.

GRATITUDE IS THE MASTER KEY

Unveiling a Life of Abundance

"Gratitude awakens us to the richness of the present moment, inviting us to savour the beauty that surrounds us and the miracles that unfold within us."

By incorporating a daily gratitude practice, you can cultivate a mindset of abundance, foster a positive outlook, and enhance your overall well-being. Even if you don't use any lesson in this book. Use the one I am about to share. This has the power to change your life.

I. Understanding the Power of Gratitude

A. Exploring the Definition and Concept of Gratitude:

Gratitude is more than just saying "thank you." It's a mindset and a way of being. In this section, we will delve into what gratitude truly means and how it can shift your perspective. Gratitude involves acknowledging the good in your life, recognizing the blessings, and appreciating both the big and small things that bring you joy. It has the power to shift your energy completely.

B. Recognizing the Numerous Benefits of Practicing Gratitude:

Did you know that gratitude has a profound impact on your mental, emotional, and physical well-being? From reducing stress and anxiety to improving sleep quality and boosting overall happiness, practicing gratitude has a wide range of positive effects.

C. Understanding How Gratitude Can Shape Your Identity:

Gratitude has the power to transform how you see yourself and how others perceive you. By cultivating a grateful mindset, you can boost your authority and self-confidence. We'll discuss how gratitude empowers you to make fearless decisions, own your strengths, and navigate life's challenges with resilience and grace.

2) The Science Behind Gratitude

A. Examining the Psychological and Physiological Effects of Gratitude:

Gratitude is not just a feel-good sentiment; it has real, measurable effects on our brains and bodies. Let's explore the psychological and physiological impact of gratitude, such as improved mood, increased resilience, and enhanced overall well-being. Understanding the science behind gratitude can help solidify its importance in your daily life.

1. Improved Mood: Research has shown that expressing gratitude can lead to improved mood and increased happiness. In a study published in the Journal of Personality and Social Psychology, participants who engaged in a gratitude exercise reported higher levels of positive emotions and greater life satisfaction compared to those who did not engage in the exercise.

2. Decreased Depression and Anxiety: Gratitude practices have been found to be effective in reducing symptoms of depression and anxiety. A study published in Behaviour Research and Therapy found that individuals with clinical depression who wrote letters of gratitude experienced a significant reduction in depressive symptoms and increased levels of well-being compared to those in the control group.

3. Increased Resilience: Gratitude has been linked to increased resilience, which is the ability to bounce back from adversity. A study published in Emotion found that individuals who engaged in gratitude exercises showed higher resilience levels and were better able to cope with stress and trauma.

4. Better Sleep: Expressing gratitude before bedtime has been associated with improved sleep quality. According to a study published in Applied Psychology: Health and Well-Being, individuals who wrote down things they were grateful for before going to bed experienced longer and better-quality sleep compared to those who did not engage in the gratitude exercise.

5. Physical Health Benefits: Gratitude practices have been linked to a range of physical health benefits. A study published in Personality and Individual Differences found that individuals who reported higher levels of gratitude had lower levels of inflammation, improved heart rate variability, and healthier lipid profiles, which are factors associated with cardiovascular health.

6. Increased Prosocial Behaviour: Grateful individuals tend to exhibit more prosocial behaviour, such as kindness and helping others. A study published in the Journal of Positive Psychology found that people who regularly practiced gratitude were more likely to engage in altruistic acts and were perceived as more helpful by others.

Incorporating gratitude into daily life through practices like keeping a gratitude journal or expressing appreciation to others can have profound and measurable benefits.

3) Cultivating a Daily Gratitude Practice

A. Creating Your Gratitude Ritual:

Establishing a consistent gratitude practice is key to reaping its benefits. Allow me to guide you through different methods for expressing gratitude, such as keeping a gratitude journal, practicing mindfulness, or engaging in gratitude meditation. Find a ritual that resonates with you and commit to incorporating it into your daily routine.

Here are some examples of gratitude rituals that you can adopt

1. Gratitude Journal: Write down three things you are grateful for each day before going to bed.

2. Gratitude Jar: Write down moments of gratitude on small pieces of paper and place them in a jar. Read them at the end of each week or month.

3. Gratitude Walk: Take a mindful walk outdoors, focusing on things you are grateful for in your surroundings.

4. Gratitude Letter: Write a heartfelt letter expressing gratitude to someone who has positively impacted your life.

5. Gratitude Meditation: Set aside a few minutes each day to sit quietly and reflect on the things you are grateful for.

6. Gratitude Buddy: Find a gratitude partner and share three things you are grateful for with each other every day.

7. Gratitude Board: Create a visual board where you can pin or stick images or words representing what you are grateful for.

8. Gratitude Ritual at Mealtimes: Before eating, take a moment to express gratitude for the food, the people who prepared it, and the nourishment it provides. This ritual is followed by the Japanese before they have their food.

9. Gratitude Affirmations: Repeat positive affirmations focused on gratitude, such as "I am grateful for the abundance in my life" or "I appreciate the small joys that come my way."

10. Gratitude Reflection: Before going to sleep, reflect on three good things that happened during the day and express gratitude for them.

Choose a gratitude ritual that resonates with you and fits well into your daily routine. Remember, consistency is key to cultivating a gratitude practice and experiencing its benefits.

4) The Transformative Power of Gratitude

A. Shifting Your Perspective:

Gratitude has the power to reframe your perspective on life. It can help you find silver linings in challenging situations, reframe setbacks as opportunities for growth, and cultivate an attitude of optimism.

B. Practicing Gratitude in Difficult Times:

Gratitude is not limited to times of abundance; it can be particularly impactful during difficult periods. According to research published in the Journal of Positive Psychology, individuals who practiced gratitude during difficult times reported a shift in perspective, viewing challenges as opportunities for growth and finding silver linings in tough situations.

Key Takeaways:

Gratitude is more than a simple "thank you." It is a mindset and a way of being that involves acknowledging and appreciating the blessings in your life, big and small.

Practicing gratitude has numerous benefits, including reduced stress, improved sleep, enhanced well-being, and increased self-confidence.

The science behind gratitude reveals its psychological and physiological impact, reinforcing its importance in daily life.

Cultivating a daily gratitude practice requires creating a ritual, fostering mindfulness, and expressing gratitude to others.

Gratitude has the transformative power to shift your perspective, find silver linings in difficult situations, and guide you through challenging times.

Action Points:

Start a gratitude journal and write down three things you're grateful for each day.

Practice a five-minute gratitude meditation every morning or evening, focusing on the blessings in your life.

Express gratitude to someone who has made a positive impact on your life through a heartfelt note, message, or face-to-face conversation.

Take regular moments throughout the day to pause, breathe, and appreciate the present moment and the beauty around you.

During difficult times, challenge yourself to find at least one thing to be grateful for each day, even if it's small.

THE FINAL PAGE

Embrace Your True Identity and Soar to New Heights*

"As this chapter draws to a close, remember that the real beauty lies not in the ending but in the infinite possibilities that bloom from the seeds of transformation you have planted."

Dear Creative Problem-solvers and Growth-oriented Achievers,

Congratulations! You have journeyed through the seven transformative steps of this book, discovering the true essence of who you are and unleashing the powerful force within you. As you reach the end of this life-changing book, let your heart swell with pride for the remarkable progress you've made. Your unwavering determination to build your identity and authority, fearlessly take your own decisions, and rewrite your life story is truly commendable.

The Journey: Seven Transformative Steps towards a Life of Purpose and Fulfillment

Step 1: Empowering Yourself for Personal Growth and Independence

Remember the moment you decided to take charge of your life? That was the spark that ignited the flame of empowerment within you. Embrace your unique strengths and talents, and never shy away from investing in your personal growth. You are the architect of your destiny, and with each small step, you are creating a grand masterpiece.

Step 2: Cultivating Meaningful Relationships and Connections

Through this journey, you've realized the value of meaningful connections. Nurture these bonds, for they are the pillars of your support system. Surround yourself with people who lift you higher, celebrate your victories, and stand by you during challenges. Together, you'll create a tapestry of love, understanding, and growth.

Step 3: Prioritizing Well-being and Finding Balance in Your Life

In the hustle and bustle of life, do not forget to prioritize your well-being. Self-care is not selfish; it is a crucial step in your journey towards self-discovery. Embrace balance, and you'll witness the magic that unfolds when you take care of your body, mind, and soul.

Step 4: Overcoming Challenges and Embracing Fearlessness

Challenges will come knocking on your door, but do not fear them. Rather, greet them with open arms, for they are the stepping stones to your success. With each hurdle you conquer, you'll become stronger, wiser, and more resilient. Fearlessness is not the absence of fear; it is the courage to face fear head-on and emerge victorious.

Step 5: Building a Supportive Network and Engaging in Community

A supportive network is a lifeline in your journey. Together, you form a tight-knit community that uplifts, inspires, and empowers one another. Reach out and lend a helping hand to those around you, for in doing so, you'll discover the immense joy of collective growth.

Step 6: Achieving Financial Freedom and Security

Financial freedom is not just about accumulating wealth; it is about gaining control over your life and choices. Learn to manage your finances wisely, invest in your dreams, and secure your future. As you achieve financial stability, you'll have the freedom to explore endless possibilities. You will also become a support system to your ecosystem. Create a win-win situation for all.

Step 7: Nurturing a Mindset of Abundance and Positivity

Your mindset is the compass that guides you through life's journey. Cultivate a mindset of abundance and positivity, and you'll attract boundless opportunities and happiness. Gratitude is the key that unlocks the door to a fulfilling life. Celebrate every little success and cherish the lessons learned from setbacks.

Dear Empowered Homemakers, this is not just the conclusion of a book; it is the beginning of an extraordinary chapter in your life. As you stand at this crossroad, remember that you possess all the tools you need to **rewrite your life story**. Embrace your newfound identity and authority, and watch how you transform the ordinary into the extraordinary.

In times of doubt, remember the seven steps that have become your guiding stars. Look back on the progress you've made and draw strength from it.

Believe in yourself and your limitless potential, for you are capable of achieving greatness beyond your wildest dreams.

May your journey be filled with unwavering determination, endless love, and boundless joy. Your impact as growth-minded homemakers extends far beyond the walls of your homes. You are inspiring future generations, breaking barriers, and shaping a better world.

Now, go forth, my dear change-makers, and shine your light brightly. The world eagerly awaits the magnificent transformations you are about to unleash. Be fearless, be bold, and let your authentic self-soar to new heights. Your story is being rewritten, and it is nothing short of extraordinary.

With heartfelt admiration and unwavering belief,

Lot's of love

Farida Bharmal

The Personality Designer

CONGRATULATIONS!

Dear Reader,

Congratulations on reaching the remarkable milestone of finishing your book! What an incredible achievement that deserves celebration.

As a token of appreciation, I'm delighted to offer you a free gift: the "Building Self-Confidence Workbook" in PDF format.

Scan this QR code to access your free eBook